CUBAN
COCKTAILS

★ ★ ★ ★ ★ ★

Cantineros proudly pose at their stations in one of Havana's numerous bars.

CUBAN COCKTAILS

DRINKS & THE CANTINEROS
WHO CREATED THEM
FROM CUBA'S GOLDEN
AGE OF COCKTAILS

BY
ANISTATIA MILLER
& JARED BROWN

MIXELLANY

MIXELLANY LIMITED

First edition

ISBN 13: 978-1-907434-10-5

British Library Cataloguing in Publication Data.
A catalogue record for this book is available from the British Library.

DEDICATION

We write this dedication with debts of gratitude to two master cantineros who were generous with their most perishable of assets: their time.

To the late Elio Moya: You taught us so much, so quickly when in 2008 we met.

To the late José Luis "Josep" Maruenda: Along with your wonderful wife, Maria Dolores Boadas, you made our first night in Barcelona, in 2006, among the most memorable of our lives. And your hidden bar, Caribbean Club, was a trove of Cuban rum history. Your hands and shaker still appear behind us in our publicity photo, and your photograph will forever hang in our house.

We dedicate this book to these two dearly departed gentlemen bartenders, and to all who are truly passionate about rum, rum drinks and the bartending profession.

Cantinero Elio Moya in his later years.

CONTENTS

PART ONE ★ ★ ★

A Golden Recipe for a Golden Age

INTRODUCTION

The Golden Age of the Cocktail. People usually use this term to refer to a time when bartending in America hit new heights between 1880 and 1919 in the hands of Harry Johnson, Willy Schmitt, and others equipped with copies of Jerry Thomas's book plus recipes and concepts imported from Europe—people who today's bartenders know as their forefathers. Importing their cultural influences, they crafted a symphony of tastes and service standards that are still used today.

A golden age occurred in Europe, too, between 1862 and 1950. Passionate protagonists of the cocktail plied their craft from London to Paris and Deauville, from Venice and Istanbul to Singapore and Tokyo. Some honed their skills in the US, only to return home as the cocktail's champions when Prohibition closed America's bars. But another golden age arose in the Caribbean, in Cuba, in Havana, during those same years. And a new term defined its adepts—cantineros.

British journalist and author Basil Woon called Havana the "Little Paris of the Caribbean" in his 1928 travelogue *When It's Cocktail Time in Cuba.* Chic, sophisticated, cosmopolitan, the city was a playground for the world's elite, and a proving ground for a groundbreaking generation of bartenders.[1] By the time Woon discovered their talents, pioneer cantineros had already beguiled the world's A-listers with Cuban rum, masterfully crafting classics that eventually circumnavigated the globe.

How did Cuba's bartending scene become a key component in the development of classic cocktail culture, begetting the Tiki family

---

1   Woon, Basil, *When It's Cocktail Time in Cuba* (New York: Horace Liveright, 1928).

of mixed drinks as well as the elegant mixing style found in Spanish bars—especially Barcelona? Why did Cuba attract some of the world's legendary bar talent, including Eddie Woelke and Fred Kaufman?

This is where our story begins.

In the prologue to his second book of poems *Motivos de Son*, Nicolás Guillén proudly proclaimed:

> The spirit of Cuba is mestizo. And from the spirit to the skin the definitive colour comes to us. Some day they will say: 'Cuban colour.'[2]

Cuba itself is like a well-balanced cocktail. This unique homogenous society was created by the marriage of Spanish and African cultures with splashes and dashes of other influences—from indigenous Caribbean tribes, British and French colonists, indentured Chinese workers, Arabs, North Americans, and South Americans. This blend has shaped the island's heart and soul.

So what's the recipe?

---

2 Guillén, Nicholás, *Motivos de Son* (Havana: Bouze y Ca, 1930).

Customers in a Havana café during the early twentieth century.

Chapter 1
★ ★ ★ ★

The Essential First Ingredient:
Ice

Havana's bodega/bars and barmen were among the earliest adopters of crystal-clear, commercial ice in drinks. Frederic Tudor, "the Ice King", was the first person to successfully export ice harvested from New England lakes to the rest of the world. The first shipment arrived in Martinique in 1806 and the following year Cuba became an eager recipient. Fresh juices made from the island's bounty of pineapples, key limes, and coconuts were made even more enticing when chilled with this precious commodity.

Ice contributed to the success of the bodega La Piña de Plata [The Silver Pineapple], serving VIPs and politicians who frequented the nearby El Capitolio from its opening in 1820, and other spots where locals and tourists alike learnt to appreciate Cuba's hot, tropical climate whilst sipping a refreshing, thirst quenching drink.

Canchánchara and Saoco made with the local rum became even more enticing with the addition of ice and became indigenous classics when Cuban rum came into its own. But these were not the drinks that brought this spirit style into the global drinks repertoire.

SAOCO

'n a tall (10 oz) highball glass: 2 oz Havana Club Light Dry, 4 oz coconut water (the liquid inside the coconut, not the milk or cream extracted from the meat), ice cubes or cracked ice. Stir and serve with a straw' (This drink looks and tastes better if served in the coconut itself.[3]

---

3   Zumbado, Hector. *The Barman's Sixth Sense* (Havana: Cubaexport, 1981)

Chapter 2
★ ★ ★ ★

A Late Arrival
& Second Essential Ingredient:
# Cuban Rum

Cuban rum was a very late entry to the cocktail world for two reasons.

Despite its prominence in mixed drinks during the 1900s through to today (and despite the battles waged by rum producers to maintain their hierarchal prominence behind the bar), Cuban rums had stiff competition to gain share with bar owners and with customers from the late 1700s well into the 1900s.

In the US, there were few cocktails or mixed drinks that were created using Scotch whisky or Irish whiskey during the 1800s: domestic Bourbon and rye were the preferred calls. The same held true for rums. The New England rum industry was well established. Medford rum had been produced, since 1647, in Massachusetts.

It was cheaper than any import. The supply was abundant until the Great Molasses Flood of 1919, followed by the start of Prohibition.

The popularity of Jamaican and Barbados rums dates back at least to George Washington's formative years—well before the 1776 American Revolution. The first US president campaigned with barrels of Barbados rum when he first stood for office in the Virginia colony as well as when he campaigned for the presidential seat. His wife Martha was famed for her Barbados Rum Punch.

Secondly, the style that we now recognise as authentic Cuban rum did not develop until technological advances such as Charles Derosne's charcoal filtration machine arrived on the island. (Derosne personally installed his invention, in 1841, in a sugar mill in the Matanzas region and trained technicians to operate it. Even before Derosne's inventions were patented and sold in the US, they were fully operational in Cuba.)

This improvement in sugar refinement was adapted by distillers simply because many of the companies that serviced the plantations maintained both operations under the same roof.

It took another two decades to finesse the process into the distiller's art that is unique to the island, and it was nearly forty years before the quality and beauty that is Cuban rum reached the cocktail world.

Jerry Thomas only prescribed the use of Jamaica and Santa Cruz rums in his 1862 edition of *The Bar-Tender's Guide*, the earliest book known to contain cocktail recipes.

In the 1882 edition of his *Bartenders' Manual*, Harry Johnson makes reference to rums that every well-stocked bar should have: Jamaica Rum, Medford Rum, St Croix Rum were the most commonly cited save for Hot English Rum Punch which called for Old English-style rum.

This was not an oversight. It was simply that the spirit that we now identify as being authentic Cuban rum was still in its infancy and was not yet recognised for its unique characteristics and value as an export until the 1898 Spanish-American War.

By the time those early adopters of drink—the US military forces—arrived in Cuba, the island's bars were well supplied with frosty-cold, clear ice, manufactured by Cuba's growing network of commercial ice houses. This distinctive, charcoal-filtered, blended rum flowed like water from the island's numerous distilleries, which sold more domestically than they did internationally as national consumption rose into the millions of litres.

The ice and the perfect rum were only the beginning of a recipe for an enduring drinks repertoire.

Chapter 3
★ ★ ★ ★

A Splash of Spanish Style:
Don Narciso, Maragato & Constante

Since the first moment that Christopher Columbus landed on Cuba in 1492 and claimed the island on behalf of King Ferdinand of Spain, these two countries have had an everlasting bond. Settlers quickly made their way across the Atlantic after this new world was discovered. And by the 1500s, Spanish culture was woven into the Cuban fabric.

The focus of our particular attention, however, is when Catalan emigrants from Spain's northeastern coast arrived in Cuba. That is when the bartending profession received its first injection of Spanish style.

DON NARCISO SALA PARERA

The old standby, La Florida, gained an even greater reputation when Catalan emigrant Don Narciso Sala Parera took over ownership, in 1898, and changed its name from La Piña de Plata to La Florida. Seemingly overnight, the bodega was transformed.

Although most of Havana's cantineros made their cocktails icy cold by shaking them in a two-part or three-part shaker set, Parera trained his staff to mix their drinks the old fashioned way, the Catalan way, letting the liquid fall gracefully between two mixing glasses held one high above the other whilst holding back the ice with a julep strainer in the higher of the two glasses.

Parera's cousin Miguel Boadas carried this tradition back with him when he in turn emigrated, in 1925, to Barcelona. Within a few years Boadas opened the city's first cocktail establishment Bar Boadas and one of the Spain's earliest locations dedicated to serving cocktails.[4]

---

4   Font, Alberto Gómez. "From Chicote to the Kalimocho: A Century of Cocktails", *Mixologist: The Journal of the European Cocktail, Volume 3* (London: Mixellany Limited, 2009)

EMILIO "MARAGATO" GONZÁLEZ

Spain was the ancestral home for many famed cantineros such as Emilio "Maragato" González. From the moment he arrived in Havana, in 1910, until his death in 1940, Maragato elevated the standards by which Cuban cocktails were made: Shaker at the ready, elegantly dressed in his white jacket, Maragato captured the hearts of every and anyone to came to pay homage to this cocktail master. In his capable hands, the Daiquirí and the Maragato Special were served by the hundreds to Hotel Florida's and Hotel Plaza's elite clientele.

MARAGATO SPECIAL

¼ orange juice
¼ French vermouth
¼ Italian vermouth
¼ rum
juice of a half lemon
dashes of maraschino
Shake ingredient over ice and strain into a cocktail glass.[5]

---

5   Sanchez, Hilario Alonso. *El Arte del Cantinero: Los Vinos y Los Licores* (Havana: P. Hernandez y Cia, S. Inc., 1948)

CONSTANTINO RIBALAIGUA VERT

Three blocks away from the Hotel Florida, another Catalan native positioned both the Daiquirí and the cantinero's profession on the centre stage. Taking a bartending job, in 1914, it took Constantino Ribalaigua Vert only four years to climb the ladder from cantinero to proprietor of La Florida, which he renamed El Floridita.

"Like a juggler coming into the ring, with black trousers, white shirt, string tie, tuxedo jacket, and an apron", Constante performed his magic before a star-studded audience from the Duke of Windsor and philosopher Jean-Paul Sartre, to novelist Ernest Hemingway and a host of Hollywood screen stars.

Constante brandished the key limes he took from his special cache. He squeezed them high above the bar, like a magician pulling a rabbit from his hat. Actress Ava Gardner swooned at the sight.

His contribution to the development of the Daiquirí will be discussed later in this book.

Spain was not the only nation that influenced the Cuban cocktail mix. The next distinctive flavour hailed from Germany.

Chapter 4
★ ★ ★ ★

A Dash of German Precision:
Eddie

Prohibition closed the curtain on America's Golden Age of Cocktails, but not before a young, well-trained generation of bartenders honed their skills behind the mahogany at landmark spots such as the Hoffman House and Hotel Knickerbocker. Many of America's bar legends from that golden era were born in Germany such as Harry Johnson and Willy Schmidt, or were first-generation German-Americans such as Henry C Ramos and Eddie Woelke.

Born in Philadelphia in 1877, Eddie worked in of the world's finest watering holes. From the Germantown Cricket Club in his hometown he made his way to the Plaza

Athenée in Paris, where he also met his wife Marcelle. Returning to the US, he took a post in New York's Hotel Knickerbocker, in 1906, with a young Harry Craddock (later of Savoy Hotel fame) and restaurant/bar manager James B Regan.

When hotel's owner John Jacob Astor IV died in the tragic maiden voyage of the *Titanic*, on 15 April 1912, the hotel was handed over to his son Vincent. Possibly the change of ownership did not suit Woelke, who took a post down the street, in 1913, at the New York Biltmore Hotel which opened on New Year's Day.

Just as Prohibition loomed on the horizon, luck sided with Eddie.

The Biltmore's owners John McEntee Bowman and Charles Francis Flynn had purchased the Sevilla Hotel on Calle Trocadero in Havana, in 1919, and renamed it the Sevilla-Biltmore Hotel. Eddie was transferred there as part of the opening team.

EL PRESIDENTE & PRESIDENTE MACHADO

General Mario García Menocal y Deop had been Cuba's president since his election in 20 May 1913. He was still in office when the hotel began to welcome dignitaries, celebrities, and masters of industry who visited this isle of tropical hospitality. Is it possible that Eddie put this drink on the menu to honour a visit from El Presidente?

According to some sources, the drink was first created at the Bar Vista Alegre on Calle Belascoaín, which was built sometime after 1909 when the Malécon's construction reach that area.

It is possible that word of the drink reached Woelke, who finessed it and popularised amongst his elite clientele. And local lore has frequently noted that this was the politician's favourite recipe before 1921, when he was voted out of office.

When the Sevilla-Biltmore's 10-storey tower wing and grand ballroom were added, in 1924, Eddie left the renovations behind and moved on to the Casino Nacional. (Some people say he also did a stint at the Havana American Jockey Club).

Once again, who knows if he was responsible? But when President Gerardo Machado was voted into office the following year, El Presidente was slightly modified and renamed Presidente Machado.

A slim volume titled *El Arte de Hacer un Cocktail y Algo Mas* was published in Havana, in 1927, by the Compañia Cervecera International SA. There we find Eddie's Presidente as well as a Presidente Machado! What's the difference? Dashes of both grenadine and curaçao are used to enhance the marriage of white rum and dry vermouth in the Machado.[6]

EL PRESIDENTE (1927 VERSION)

½ rum
½ French vermouth
dashes of grenadine
Stir over ice and strain into a cocktail glass. Garnish with an orange peel.[7]

PRESIDENTE MACHADO (1927 VERSION)

½ rum
½ French vermouth
dashes of grenadine
dashes of curaçao
Stir over ice and strain into a cocktail glass. Garnish with an orange peel.[8]

Basil Woon gave Woelke's El Presidente the highest praise back in 1928, noting that:

It is the aristocrat of cocktails and is the one preferred by the better class of Cuban.[9]

---

6   *El Arte de Hacer un Cocktail y Algo Mas* (Havana: Compañia Cervecera International SA, 1927; Cheltenham: Mixellany Limited, 2011)

7   *El Arte de Hacer un Cocktail y Algo Mas* (Havana: Compañia Cervecera International SA, 1927; Cheltenham: Mixellany Limited, 2011)

8   *El Arte de Hacer un Cocktail y Algo Mas* (Havana: Compañia Cervecera International SA, 1927; Cheltenham: Mixellany Limited, 2011)

9   Woon, Basil, *When It's Cocktail Time in Cuba* (New York: Horace Liveright, 1928)

We know that Machado himself was proud enough of his version to present it to another dignitary: Calvin Coolidge, who was US President during the height of Prohibition. The press was at the scene:

> ...although the state dinner given by President Machado of Cuba at the presidential palace last night in honor of President Coolidge was exceedingly wet, starting with a fiery 'presidente cocktail' and ending with fine old 1811 brandy, guests at the dinner insisted that President Coolidge did not drink any of the wines or liquors.[10]

American newspapermen at the scene tried to pry more details from guests and officials. But none were forthcoming. So they declared in their columns—without witnessing the dinner—that Coolidge had scrupulously abstained.

El Presidente's and Presidente Machado's popularity continued in Havana's bars even after, in 1933, the Cuban president was exiled.

Constantino Ribalaigua Vert preferred to have his staff garnish it with a cocktail cherry.

---

10   "President Leaves Cuba for Florida", *The Independent* (St Petersburg FL), evening edition, 17 January 1928.

EL PRESIDENTE
(LA FLORIDA VERSION)

½ Chambery Vermouth.

½ Bacardi.

½ Teaspoonful of Curacao.

Crushed ice.

Cool well and strain.

Serve with cherries and a peel of orange.[11]

> Charles H Baker Jr, author of *The Gentleman's Companion*, discovered the drink at Bar La Florida later in that decade.[12]

HABANA PRESIDENTE

1 pony each of Bacardi Gold Seal, and dry French vermouth, into a bar glass with cracked ice. Donate 1 tsp grenadine and the same of curaçao. Stir and serve in a Manhattan glass with a scarlet cherry for garnish. FInally twist a curl of yellow orange peel over the top so that the oil strikes the suraface of the drink, then drop the peel in…

> The Cuban bartenders' association took a slight step back to Woelke's recipe and a baby step forward when they standardised recipe in their 1948 edition of *El Arte del Cantinero*.

---

11   *Bar La Florida* (Havana: La Florida, 1936)

12   Baker, Charles H, Jr, *The Gentleman's Companion: Volume II, Being an Exotic Drinking Book or, Around the Word with Jigger, Beaker and Flask* (New York: Derrydale Press, 1939).

PRESIDENTE (1948 VERSION)

½ vermouth Chambery
½ rum
spoonful of grenadine
Stir over ice and strain into a cocktail glass. Garnish
with a cherry and an orange twist.[13]

> After Prohibition was repealed in 1933,
> Eddie returned to New York where he presided
> at the Hotel Weylin Bar, bringing with him his
> talent for working with Cuban rum, which is
> documented in his 1936 book *The Barman's
> Mentor.*

---

13   Sanchez, Hilario Alonso. *El Arte del Cantinero: Los Vinos y Los
Licores* (Havana: P. Hernandez y Cia, S. Inc., 1948)

The Hotel Sevilla-Biltmore's 1924 makover included a multistoried addition plus a rooftop ballroom.

Chapter 5
★ ★ ★ ★

A Dash of British Panache:
Fred

Woelke shared the mahogany at the
Sevilla-Biltmore with Fred Kaufman. He may
never have written a cocktail book but Basil
Woon immortalised Kaufman's efforts:

Presiding over the long mahogany are the two whose
acquaintance it is probable you will make first of all,
for they are the bartenders: Eddie Woehlke [sic], who
came to Havana from New York via Paris, who has
a French wife with a modiste's shop, Marcelle's, of
her own in New York, and whom pre-war residents
of Paris will recall as thirst-dispenser at the Plaza-
Athenée and Fred Kaufman, originally of Liverpool,
but a traveler of the Tropics so long that he talks
English with a Spanish accent. Kaufman is never

happy unless he is on an island. He was born on
one, and has since worked in Funchal, Madeira,
and the Canary islands. Kaufman is the inventor of
several cocktails in which pineapple juice is the chief
ingredient…

…

The Mary Pickford invented during a visit to Havana of
the screen favourite by Fred Kaufman…[14]

MARY PICKFORD (1928 VERSION)

2/3 pineapple juice
1/3 rum
1 dash grenadine
Shake ingredients over ice and strain into a cocktail
glass.[15]

More often than not, another drink
from the era—the Dorothy Gish Cocktail,
named after another silent film star—is also
attributed to Woelke, not Kaufman. But the
profile alludes to Kaufman's authorship.

DOROTHY GISH NO. 2 COCKTAIL
(1948 VERSION)

½ oz white rum
½ oz apricot brandy
2 spoonfuls orange juice

---

14   Woon, Basil, *When It's Cocktail Time in Cuba* (New York: Horace
Liveright, 1928)

15   Woon, Basil, *When It's Cocktail Time in Cuba* (New York: Horace
Liveright, 1928)

2 spoonfuls pineapple juice
Shake ingredients over ice and strain into a cocktail
glass.[16]

Some reports say that Kaufman eventually took a post at the Hotel Nacional de Cuba (as opposed to Woelke working at the Casino Nacional) when it opened its doors on 30 December 1930. But then, there has obviously been a lot of crossover between Woelke's and Kaufman's careers reported in the media.

But when you look at the ingredients in the Nacional Cocktail, they bear the mark of the Kaufman touch.

NACIONAL COCKTAIL (1948 VERSION)

½ rum
¼ pineapple juice
¼ apricot brandy
dashes of lemon juice
Shake ingredients over ice. Strain into a cocktail
glass. Garnish with a pineapple wedge.[17]

16   Sanchez, Hilario Alonso. *El Arte del Cantinero: Los Vinos y Los Licores* (Havana: P. Hernandez y Cia, S. Inc., 1948)

17   Sanchez, Hilario Alonso. *El Arte del Cantinero: Los Vinos y Los Licores* (Havana: P. Hernandez y Cia, S. Inc., 1948)

Brimming with shops and cafés
Calle Obispo was a popular
destination at the turn of the
century.

CHAPTER 6
★ ★ ★ ★

A Twist of American Know-How:
Donovan & the Economides Brothers

University of North Carolina Professor of History Louis A Pérez Jr gave the most accurate description of the American bartender invasion that struck Havana at the dawn of Prohibition:

> Unemployed bartenders and saloon keepers found jobs in Havana as bars and cabarets that closed in the United States were reopened in Cuba. William Caldwell's Neptuno Bar...Harry McCabe's Golden

Dollar Bar...Tom Morris from Cleveland owned the
American Busy Bee Bar...Pat Cody also reopened
his New York saloon, Jigg's Uptown Bar...John Moller
from Brooklyn opened Ballyhoo Bar...George harris
operated George's Winter Palace...Harry McGabe
opened the Rialto Café, along on the Prado. ...The
Seminole Café offered "nothing but genuine American
and Scotch whiskey. Best draught beer in town."[18]

The Irish-American saloon tradition
arrived on Cuban shores when Ed Donovan,
who hailed from Newark NJ moved to Havana
at the inception of Prohibition. He opened Café
Donovan behind the Telégrafo Hotel, bringing
his chairs, tables, mirrors, hanging sign, and the
bar itself to the island lock stock and barrel.
A welcome home away from home for American expats and tourists, the non-hotel style of
bartending entered into the Cuban fabric. As
reporter put it:[19]

In the meantime, Café Donovan, as the American
bar is other wise known, is headquarters for many
of the Americans living in Cuba, especially the
ones domiciled there. ... Real American cooking is
to be had and all the mixed drinks that used to be

---

18   Perez, Louis A, Jr, *On Becoming Cuban: Identity , Nationality, and
Culture* (Chapel Hill: University of North Carolina Press, 2008).

19   Woon, Basil, *When It's Cocktail Time in Cuba* (New York: Horace
Liveright, 1928); Perez, Louis A, Jr, *On Becoming Cuban: Identity ,
Nationality, and Culture* (Chapel Hill: University of North Carolina Press,
2008).

popular in the States can be obtained in their pristine perfection, for there is no lack of materials from which to compound them, nor of cunning hands to properly agitate them.[20]

The same reporter critically compared the American-owned bars to the Cuban-owned "saloons" by noting that:

It is these saloons along San Isidro street about which I particularly want to write. They have no swinging doors, like real saloons, or modern bootlegging joints in the states—in fact, they have no doors at all, the width of the bar and table space being open to the street, oftenon two sides. ...But that's not the feature of these saloons, either. It is the barmaids—comley young girls of all ages who serve the tired and thirsty traveler with the best the bar affords the minute he is seated at one of the tables.[21]

Hints of New Orleans bar culture arrived as well. Greek emigrants Constantino (aka: "Billy") and Peter Economides opened the Café Sazerac around the corner from the Inglaterra Bar & Patio around the same time.[22] Peter had

20   Murray, Chris L. "Havana Described as an Americanized Old World Place; Who Is Donovan?", *Galveston Daily News*, 6 August 1922.

21   Murray, Chris L. "Havana Described as an Americanized Old World Place; Who Is Donovan?", *Galveston Daily News*, 6 August 1922.

22   Woon, Basil, *When It's Cocktail Time in Cuba* (New York: Horace Liveright, 1928)

been Head Barman at the New Orleans Café on 42nd street near Times Square in New York,[23] where he had earned a reputation for making his own version of a Ramos Gin Fizz.

The flood of American bartenders emigrating to Cuba was noted in the stateside newspapers, literally a month after Prohibition was in full swing.

...former saloon keepers and bartenders of Chicago are going down to Havana at a rate of 12 a day, according to Jacob Poppet, internal revenue deputy collector. 'While many of these men are going down on pleasure trips," he said, "there is no doubt that some of them are going there to open saloons and prepare for the great American rush. They want to be on hand when the private stocks in the cellars are gone.[24]

It wasn't just the bartenders that were hightailing it to Havana. A few distilleries and breweries relocated to the island as well.

W.A. Kennerly relocated his Roanoke, Virginia distillery in Havana. The Havana Distilling Company— which represents considerable American capital," reported the U.S. chargé d'affaires Edward Reed—

23　Perez, Louis A, Jr, *On Becoming Cuban: Identity , Nationality, and Culture* (Chapel Hill: University of North Carolina Press, 2008).

24　"Saloon Men Go to Cuba: Twelve a Day Sail for Havana, Says United States Internal Reveneue Deputy at Chicago", *Elgin Echo*, 5 February 1920.

opened a large plant at El Cano to manufacture rye whiskey, Scotch, and other liquors. In 1920 the Cuba Cervercera Company purchased the entire factory of the U.S. Brewing Company of Chicago, increasing its production capacity to five million liters of beer daily.[25]

But as with all people who come to Cuba, these barmen were influenced at least as much as they themselves influenced local cocktail culture. They too came away with a part of Cuba in their souls, especially when a new generation of Cuban bartenders arose.

What remained after this encounter was the perfect balance, the perfect cocktail for an enduring cocktail tradition.

25   Perez, Louis A, Jr, *On Becoming Cuban: Identity , Nationality, and Culture* (Chapel Hill: University of North Carolina Press, 2008).

CLUB DE CANTINEROS D

SOCIO NUMERARIO

NUMERO DE SOCIO _318_

Elio Moya's association membership card, which identified him as a fully-qualified cantinero.

FIRMA DEL SOCIO

IOTA. PARA EJERCER LOS DERECHOS SOCIALES
ES NECESARIO LA PRESENTACION DE ESTE
CARNET Y EL RECIBO DEL MES EN CURSO.

CARNET BELMONTE MONTE 60 HABANA

Chapter 7
★ ★ ★ ★

The Perfect Blend:
Asociacion de Cantineros de Cuba

Visitors arrived from foreign shores seeking an audience with these legendary barmen. More cantineros who took pride in their craft were needed to serve the burgeoning hospitality trade of hotels, restaurants, nightclubs, private clubs, and casinos.

Aside from the Sevilla-Biltmore Hotel's acquisition and upgrade in 1919 and 1924 by John M Bowman, other American hoteliers came to Havana during the 1920s to open establishments designed to accommodate the influx of American tourists.

Walter Fletcher modelled his Hotel Plaza after New York's opulent Plaza Hotel. WT Burbridge opened the Miramar; Dwight Hughes launched the Albany Hotel; and John A Richardson welcomed guests at the Hotel Lincoln.[26]

There was also the openings of the Hotel Vanderbilt, Hotel Packard, Hotel Cecil, St Louis Hotel, Hotel Biscuit, Hotel Bristol, Savoy Hotel, Hotel Saratoga, Hotel Pacific, Hotel Palace, Boston Hotel, Miami Hotel, Hotel Parkview, Hotel Ambassador, Hotel Washington, Hotel Seminole, Clifton House, and the New Ritz Hotel.

No to be outgunned by American entrepreneurial enthusiasm, Cuban and Spanish businessmen catering to American tastes opened American-style hotels, cabarets, and eateries such as Ramón Rodríguez's Armenonville Cabaret, Segundo González's Hotel Harding, Vicente Castro's Hotel Chicago, José Valiela's Hotel Pennsylvania, Francisco García's Park House Hotel, Antonio Villanueva's Hotel Manhattan, Hosé Morgado's Hotel New York,

26   Perez, Louis A, Jr, *On Becoming Cuban: Identity , Nationality, and Culture* (Chapel Hill: University of North Carolina Press, 2008).

Teodoro Miranda's Hotel Ohio, Telégrafo Hotel, Gran Hotel América, and Hotel Almendares.[27]

Fresh from honing his skills in New Orleans, Spanish barman José Abeal opened Sloppy Joe's. Francisco and Gustavo del Barrio opened the New York Bar. Benito "Benny" Rego managed the Winter Garden Bar.[28]

What every one of these establishments promised its growing customer base was true American service, real American cuisine, real American drinks, and staff that spoke American English.

Veterans like Emilio "Maragato" González and Constantino Ribalaigua Vert heard the call for action. Havana's workforce had to give the public what they wanted: stand-ardised recipes that appealed to the American palate; service that equalled or surpassed what could be found in the US or Europe; workers that could speak English; and a healthy dose of style.[29]

Led by Maragato and Constante, the Asociacion de Cantineros de Cuba was founded, in 1924, and headquartered below Paseo del Prado in the heart of Havana's grand hotel district. Subsidised by local distilleries, brasse-ries and liquor merchants the association served

27   Perez, Louis A, Jr, *On Becoming Cuban: Identity , Nationality, and Culture* (Chapel Hill: University of North Carolina Press, 2008).

28   Perez, Louis A, Jr, *On Becoming Cuban: Identity , Nationality, and Culture* (Chapel Hill: University of North Carolina Press, 2008).

29   Personal interview with Elio Moya, 26 August 2008.

several roles: as a trade union that defended the cantineros' professional interests; as a guild that provided English courses for apprentices; as a gathering place that nurtured the health and well-being of its members with a library, a jai-alai court, billiard room, and bathing establishment.[30]

To gain a journeyman qualification, an apprentice had to learn how to mix 100 cocktails from memory. An annual competition with very strict rules assured that even master cantineros never lost their edge. They competed before a jury comprised of both industry professionals and select civilians: "new palates" who were as passionate about cocktails as the contestants. This added freshness—and an essential connection with the customers—to the proceedings.[31]

Nine years before the United Kingdom Bartenders Guild—frequently cited as the world's first bartender's association—was established by a group of London bartenders, the Asociacion de Cantineros de Cuba was already training a new generation of Cuban-born professions to live up to journalist Hector Zumbado's eloquent description:

> They have the elegance of a symphony conductor, the precision and calm of a surgeon ready to operate. They are the chemists of today, the botanists of the

---

30   Personal interview with Elio Moya, 26 August 2008.

31   Personal interview with Elio Moya, 26 August 2008.

eighteenth century, the alchemists of the Middle Ages, capable of willing the creation of cool, shining gold. They are experts in the topics of sport and international politics, but they never give in to passionate discourse. ...They need the memory of elephants for they must remember how to make, without looking them up, between 100 and 200 cocktails. ...Such a man exists. He is the Barman, imaginative and creative, a craftsman in ice, a poet of potions, imbued with a true love for his work. He has his own personality and style. He puts something of himself, of his innermost self into every drink he prepares: part of him is in it, giving it life. ...His five senses are superbly tuned. And he has a sixth sense: the sense of cocktail-making.[32]

This passion, this mastery of skills and ingredients, this formation of a new and wholly Cuban style of bartending became more than an isolated, ethnocentric pastiche. Cuban bartending in its golden age stretched out and embraced the world as entranced visitors and even a Cuban-born bartender exported this artistry to the rest of the world.

---

32   Zumbado, Hector. *The Barman's Sixth Sense* (Havana: Cubaexport, 1981)

FINE RUMS FROM DON THE BEACHCOMBER'S CELLAR

CUBA

Alvarez Carta Camp Gold	Cuba $	.40
Alvarez Carta Camp Matusalem (15 years old)	Cuba	.50
Alvarez Carta Camp Silver	Cuba	.40
Anejo	Cuba	.45
Bacardi Elixir	Cuba	.60
Bacardi 1873	Cuba	.60
Bacardi Carta de Oro	Cuba	.40
Bacardi Carta Blanca	Cuba	.40
Beachcomber's (6 years old)	Cuba	.40
Bebida	Cuba	.40
Bellow's Malecon Gold	Cuba	.40
Bellow's Malecon Silver	Cuba	.40
Bolero	Cuba	.40
Cabellero	Cuba	.40
Cubanola (12 years old)	Cuba	.60
Daiquiri	Cuba	.40
Havana Club	Cuba	.40
Palau (30 years old)	Cuba	.60
Ron Albuerne	Cuba	.40
Ron Caney	Cuba	.40
Ron el Infierno (20 years old)	Cuba	.45
Ron Superior Faraon	Cuba	.40
Royal Scarlet Carta D'oro	Cuba	.40
Sloppy Joe's Rum	Cuba	.40
Tango Superior	Cuba	.40

DEMERARA

Booker's Liqueur	Demerara	.45
Don's Private Brand 150 Proof	Demerara	.60
Ellis' Demerara 142 Proof	British Guiana	.45
Hedges & Butler	Demerara	.50
Hudson's Bay Demerara 91 Proof	British Guiana	.45
Hudson's Bay Demerara 151 Proof	British Guiana	.60
Lamb's Old Navy	British West Indies	.45
Lemon Hart 96 Proof	Demerara	.45
Lemon Hart 114 Proof	British Guiana	.60
Lemon Hart 151 Proof	British Guiana	.60
Lownde's (Don's Private Label) 96 Proof (Blended Specially for Don the Beachcomber)	Demerara	.45
Lownde's (Don's Private Label) 151 Proof	Demerara	.60
Southard's Western Pearl	Demerara	.45
Trower's Gold Lion 100 Proof	Demerara	.45
Trower's Gold Lion 151 Proof	Demerara	.60

MARTINIQUE

Alexis Godillot	Martinique	.45
Barum	Martinique	.45
Black Head Grog	Martinique	.40
Black Head Punch	Martinique	.40
Black Head Rum	Martinique	.40
Colonial Divina	Martinique	.45
Don's Private Brand	Martinique	.45
Rhum Charleston	Martinique	.45
Risetta	Martinique	.45
Usine Sainte Marie	Martinique	.45

JAMAICA

Ballantine	Jamaica $	.45
Bellow's Choicest Liqueur	Jamaica	.60
Bellow's Finest Liqueur	Jamaica	.45
Burke's (6 years old)	Jamaica	.45
Charley's Red Label	Jamaica	.45
Charley's Royal Reserve (15 years old)	Jamaica	.50
Don's Private Brand	Jamaica	.60
Ellis 148 Proof	Jamaica	.75
Finzi's Ruby	Jamaica	.45
Fulcher's	Jamaica	.45
Gilbey's Governor General	Jamaica	.45
Grange Hill	Jamaica	.45
Hedges & Butler	Jamaica	.50
Hudson's Bay 91	Jamaica	.45
Hudson's Bay 151 Proof	Jamaica	.60
Kelly's Gold Seal	Jamaica	.50
Kelly's Grande Reserve	Jamaica	.60
Kelly's Punch Rum	Jamaica	.40
Kelly's White Label	Jamaica	.45
Lamb's Golden Grove	Jamaica	.45
Lemon Hart Twenty-eight Years	Jamaica	1.00
Lemon Hart Planter's	Jamaica	.45
Lemon Hart Liqueur	Jamaica	.60
Lemon Hart V.O.	Jamaica	.45
Lownde's (Don's Private Label)	Jamaica	.45
Myer's Light Vatted	Jamaica	.45
Myer's Mona (30 years old)	Jamaica	.80
Myer's Planter's Punch (8 years old)	Jamaica	.45
Myer's V.O. (13 years old)	Jamaica	.75
Pirate Brand	Jamaica	.45
Southard's Old London Dock	Jamaica	.45
St. James Des Plantation	Jamaica	.60
Sugar Loaf	Jamaica	.60
Treasure Cove (32 years old)	Jamaica	1.25
(Oldest and Finest Jamaica Rum in the World - Natural Strength—74 Proof)		
Trower's	Jamaica	.40
White's Red Heart	Jamaica	.45
J. Wray & Nephew's Dagger Punch	Jamaica	.45
J. Wray & Nephew's Green Label	Jamaica	.40
J. Wray & Nephew's Golden Stag (6 years old)	Jamaica	.45
J. Wray & Nephew's† (3 years old)	Jamaica	.40
J. Wray & Nephew's†† (7 years old)	Jamaica	.45
J. Wray & Nephew's‡‡ (10 years old)	Jamaica	.50
J. Wray & Nephew's Special Reserve (17 years old)	Jamaica	.60
(Bottled Exclusively for Don the Beachcomber)		

PANAMA

Beachcomber's (4 years old)	Panama	.40
Gorgona	Panama	.45

DUTCH EAST INDIES

Batavia Arak	Batavia	.75

VIRGIN ISLANDS

Black Beard	Santa Cruz $
Blue Beard	Virgin Islands
Bornn's Gold Label	Virgin Islands
Clipper	Virgin Islands
Cruxan	St. Croix
El Dorado	St. Thomas
Government House Rum	Virgin Islands
La Natividad	Virgin Islands
Old St. Croix	Virgin Islands
Old St. Croix Heavy Bodied	Virgin Islands
Pirate's Gold	Virgin Islands
St. Thomas	Virgin Islands

PORTO RICO

Beachcomber's	Porto Rico
Brugal Gold Label	Porto Rico
Brugal White Label	Porto Rico
Daiquiri	Porto Rico
Don Q	Porto Rico
Pellejas Gold	Porto Rico
Pellejas Silver	Porto Rico
Ramirez Royal Superior	Porto Rico
Ron Capito	Porto Rico
Ron Moreno	Porto Rico
Ron Rey	Porto Rico

BARBADOS

Barbados Choicest Liqueur	Barbados	.7
Barbados Finest Liqueur	Barbados	.6
Cockade	Barbados	.4
Lightbourn's	Barbados	.4
Punch & Judy	Barbados	.4

FRENCH WEST INDIES

Rhum Ara	French West Indies	.4
Rhum Ito	French West Indies	.4
Rhum Negrita	East & West Indies	.4

HAITI

Rhum Sarthe	Haiti	.4

TRINIDAD

Seigert's Bouquet Rum	Port of Spain	.4

U. S. A.

Beachcomber's	New Orleans	.40
Pontalba	Louisiana	.40
Felton's Crystal Springs	New England	.50
Pilgrim Rum	New England	.40
Treasure Cove (20 years old)	New England	.75

PHILIPPINES

Rhum Ayala	Philippines	.40
Rhum Tanduay	Philippines	.40

HAWAII

Waikiki Brand Rum	Hawaii	.40

PERU

Cartavio	Peru	.45

The rum list from Don the Beachcomber's Cellar featured the finest offerings from around the world.

Chapter 8
★ ★ ★ ★

A Colourful Garnish:
Donn Beach
& Trader Vic

Celebrities, international businessman, and tourists were not the only patrons during the 1920s and 1930s who marvelled at the cantineros' artistry.

The first to bring Cuban cocktails into the global limelight were the two recognised godfathers of Tiki who used more than a few of their experiences in Havana to develop this tropical style of drinks mixing.

ERNEST RAYMOND BEAUMONT GANTT

Ernest Raymond Beaumont Gantt, from Mexia TX, got his first taste of travel in September 1914 when, at seven years old he took a bus to Mandeville LA, to live with his grandfather. Before a month had past, Gantt was sailing the Gulf of Mexico and the Caribbean with his lively relative. As he reminisced in later years:

> But it was the travel that had me hook, line and sinker. I lusted for other islands far away. Islands I had only heard tales of from sailors and drunks when grandpappy and I would reach a new port, or sit in one of those old, broken-down bars Grandpappy loved in Haiti or Havana. Grandpappy was determined I would get an education equal to one provided by any university in the world, but a much more practical one.[33]

By the time Gantt left home, in 1926, to seek his fortune in the world, he had already experienced Havana's bars and sampled a few of its drinks. By the time he finished scouring the South Pacific and landed, in December 1931, in Hollywood, he had assimilated enough Cuban culture to incorporate it seamlessly into

---

33   Bitner, Arnold, *Scrounging the Islands with the Legendary Don the Beachcomber: Host to Diplomat, Beachcomber, Prince and Pirate* (Bloomington, IN: iUniverse, 2007)

the establishment he opened, in 1933, Don's Beachcomber Café.

Tiki was born.

The Zombie and Cuban Daiquirí were Gantt's afternoon sips for Hollywood's elite whilst Beachcomber's Gold and Beachcomber's Daiquirí were the sunset serves.[34]

He even added a Royal Daiquirí. Such was the power of the Daiquirí. It titillated American palates during the years between the two world wars and Gantt created variation to suit every mood.

ROYAL DAIQUIRI

45 ml light rum
15 ml lime juice
15 ml parfait d'amour
¼ teaspoon bar sugar
Blend with ½ scoop shaved ice in an electric drink mixer for 10 to 20 seconds. Pour into a 6-ounce champagne glass.

Gantt made regular buying trips to the Caribbean, purchasing a two-year supply of spirits from Barbados, Trinidad, Haiti, Puerto Rico, Jamaica, and Cuba to stock his rum cellar—which boasted 138 brands from 60 countries at one point—and his bar, which listed 60 of his

34   Bitner, Arnold, *Scrounging the Islands with the Legendary Don the Beachcomber: Host to Diplomat, Beachcomber, Prince and Pirate* (Bloomington, IN: iUniverse, 2007)

original tropical rum drinks. His dedication to this spirit was such that, in 1939, the industry bestowed upon him the title Ambassador of Rum.[35]

With the opening of his Chicago restaurant in 1940 in the fashionable Golden Coast, Gantt became the world's largest purchaser of Caribbean rums, serving over 325,000 cases in 1945 alone. He later recalled: "I have always claimed that rum holds certain therapeutic values and is the purest spirit made, the greatest of all drinks because it is distilled from sugar cane, and is easily assimilated into the body's system."[36]

Between 1934 and 1979, Beach spread the word about Tiki from coast to coast, opening Don the Beachcomber restaurants not only in Los Angeles (Hollywood), but in Aurora CO; Chicago IL; Corona del Mar CA; Dallas TX; Denver CO; Honolulu HI; Houston TX; Las Vegas NV; Malibu CA; Marina del Rey CA; Oxnard CA; Palm Springs CA; St Paul MN; two in San Diego CA; Santa Barbara CA; Santa Clara CA; Seattle WA; Waikiki HI; the Disney California Adventure Park; and West Lafayette LA.

---

35 Bitner, Arnold, *Scrounging the Islands with the Legendary Don the Beachcomber: Host to Diplomat, Beachcomber, Prince and Pirate* (Bloomington, IN: iUniverse, 2007)

36 Bitner, Arnold, *Scrounging the Islands with the Legendary Don the Beachcomber: Host to Diplomat, Beachcomber, Prince and Pirate* (Bloomington, IN: iUniverse, 2007)

Thanks to the Tiki revival, three locations are still in operation, at the Royal Kona Resort and the Royal Lahaina Resort in Hawaii, and one in Huntington Beach CA.

Gantt wasn't the only person to champion Caribbean rums, Cuban classic cocktails, and the tropical lifestyle in post-Prohibition America. Up north, in the San Francisco Bay area there was his friend/rival Vic Bergeron.

VICTOR JULES BERGERON JR

Vic Bergeron's first encounter with Cuban cocktails in Havana didn't occur as early in life or as colourfully Gantt's. He opened Hinky Dink's on 17 November 1934 in Oakland CA, along with his wife Esther Lynn. And as he admitted in later years:

> Although I knew quite a bit about cooking and could make all the routine cocktails, I didn't know very much about concocting fancy drinks, especially those with a tropical flavour. And this was an area where I felt real imagination could be employed—and lots of fun could be had—in mixing and serving drinks."[37]

---

37   Begeron, Victor, *Frankly Speaking: Trader Vic's Own Story* (New York: Doubleday, 1973)

After two long hard years building up the business, the couple packed their bags and headed to New Orleans. After learning a few tropical drinks from Albert Martin, owner of the Bon Ton Bar on Magazine Street, they headed south to Havana.

Bergeron walked into La Florida where he introduced himself to head bartender Constantino Rapalo [sic] and asked him how to make some of the bar's famous drinks.

When I went back to Oakland, I started to mix several different drinks. I used the La Florida [Rum Daisy] Cocktail, the La Florida Daiquirí, and a Planter's Punch, along with some of the drinks Albert Martin had shown me. And we went to work and made up a lot of new ones. Drinks that would sell in America."[38]

LA FLORIDA RUM DAISY

1 glass cracked ice
1 dash Angostura bitters
½ tsp yellow chartreuse
2 oz light rum
½ unsqueezed lemon peel
½ tsp bar sugar
several springs mint
2 cherries and fruits in season

---

38   Begeron, Victor, *Frankly Speaking: Trader Vic's Own Story* (New York: Doubleday, 1973)

Build in the glass of cracked ice; stir and serve.[39]

When Hinky Dink's was reopened as Trader Vic's, in 1937, classic Cuban cocktails and Americanised Cuban drinks were on the menu.

Within a few years, Tiki was well on its way. Vic reached further than his friend/rival Gantt, opening restaurants in Beverly Hills CA, Boston MA, Chicago IL, Dallas TX, Detroit MI, Houston TX, Kansas City KS, London UK, Los Angeles CA, Munich (Germany), New York NY, San Juan PR, and then Vic's love of Cuban flavors came full-circle when Conrad Hilton asked him to open a Trader Vic's, in 1958, at the hotelier's newest venture, the Havana Hilton.[40]

Today, there are still Trader Vic's restaurants in Beverly Hills (Mai Tai Lounge) CA; the original location in Emeryville CA; Los Angeles CA; Palo Alto CA; Atlanta GA; Sarasota FL; Portland OR; London UK; Munich GER; Hamburg (Germany); Kiev (Mai Tai Lounge) (Ukraine); Manama (Bahrain); Amman (Jordan); Muscat (Oman); Dubai Souk Madinat UAE; Dubai (Mai Tai Lounge); Al Ain UAE; Dubai Crowne Plaza UAE; Riyadh (Kingdom of Saudi Arabia); Tokyo (Japan);

---

39   Begeron, Victor, *Bartender's Guide by Trader Vic* (New York: Doubleday, 1947)

40   Begeron, Victor, *Frankly Speaking: Trader Vic's Own Story* (New York: Doubleday, 1973)

Bangkok (Thailand); and Almaty (Island Bar & Grill) (Kazakhstan).[41]

Yet Gantt and Bergeron concentrated only on the tropical drinks and rum aspects of the Cuban cantinero's art. One other disciple exported the execution, passion, and full artistic scope to Barcelona.

41   "Locations", http://www.tradervics.com/locations/locations.html

Chapter 9
★ ★ ★ ★

Artistic Presentation:
The Boadas Family

Miguel Boadas Guinart and Josefa Parera Marti, Catalan immigrants from the Spanish town of Lloret de Mar, sought a new life in Cuba. In Havana they opened a bar on Calle del Empredrado (the same narrow street where Le Bodeguita del Medio now stands) with a small apartment for themselves. Their first son, Miguel Boadas Parera, was born there on the 24th of October 1895. From the moment he opened his eyes, he was immersed in the sights and sounds of the bartender's life.

Even as a very young boy, Miguel helped his father and quickly gained an expertise at making drinks before he and his mother journeyed back to Lloret de Mar, while his father continued to run the bar in Havana.

When Miguel finished his schooling, at age 13, he returned to his father's side at the bar. Realising his son's natural talent, two years later, his father sent him to work as a fully-fledged bartender with his cousin Narciso Sala Parera, who owned La Florida.

It was Parera who taught him the finesse of throwing cocktails to chill them, a technique he quickly mastered. He took on additional work, mixing drinks in the presidential box at Havana's Jai Alai fronton (he fondly remembered serving President Mario García Menocal when he was in office from 1913 to 1921) and at the elegant bar at the Havana Yacht Club.

After owning La Florida for 20 years Parera retired, handing the business to his head bartender Constantino Ribalaigua Vert and moving back to Madrid, Spain. Boadas stayed on.

He was 31 years old when, in 1925, he decided to visit his family in Lloret de Mar. There he fell in love with Maria Ribas Utse. Love made Boadas contemplate the possibility of settling in Spain. And that is what he did: he married Maria on 10 May 1927, and they moved to Barcelona. He worked at the Moka Bar and then in other places like Nuria, Maison Dorée, the Canaletas Bar (where a special bar was designed and built for Boadas and his assistants), situated close to the Canaletas Fountain on Las Ramblas near Tallers Street.

CANALETAS COCKTAIL

1/3 Campari
1/3 Dubonnet
1/3 gin
1 dash Cointreau
Mix and serve in a cocktail glass. Garnish with a
morello cherry.

A milestone in his career was marked, on 11 October 1933, when Boadas fulfilled his life's dream and opened his own cocktail bar on Tallers Street.

BOADAS COCKTAIL

1/3 curaçao
1/3 Dubonnet
1/3 white rum
Mix and serve in a cocktail glass. Garnish with a
morello cherry.

A champion of the craft and the popularisation of cocktails in Spain, Boadas expressed his passionate feelings about the dignity of the bartending profession in the press, on radio, and later on television over the next 30 years.

Another dream came true when he founded the Club del Barman (Spanish Association of Bartenders), in 1962, which he chaired until his death.

Like the Asociacion de Cantineros de Cuba that was founded by his former bar colleague and later employer, Boadas' Club del Barman established strong ties among the growing number of Spanish bartenders, allowing them to work together for the advancement of professional dignity and the popularisation of cocktails. The association conducted cultural and fund-raising events to increase public awareness of the art of responsible drinking.

Boadas passed away, on 2 May 1967, surrounded by family: his wife, daughter Maria Dolores, and her husband José Luis "Josep" Maruenda.

In an interview conducted before his death, Miguel Boadas proclaimed:

My daughter, Maria Dolores, it was my hope that she became the first female bartender. Today, I do not think it is father's pride; I can assure she is. Regarding Josep, my son-in-law, he has assimilated so well what I tried to teach him that he is nowadays a real bartender as well. You may think that good use has been made of my legacy.[42]

---

42   Montserrat, Albert, "Miguel Boadas: The Dignified Bartender & His Daughter", *Mixologist: The Journal of the European Cocktail, Volume 3* (London: Mixellany Limited, 2008).

MARIA DOLORES

Mirroring her father's upbringing, Maria Dolores Boadas was born into the business shortly after Miguel opened the doors to Bar Boadas.

MARIA DOLORES COCKTAIL

1/3 curaçao
1/3 crème de cacao
1/3 brandy
Mix and serve in a cocktail glass. Garnish with a morello cherry.

When she was nine years old, Maria Dolores asked if she could help at the bar. (She had been playing with the glassware and bar tools for a few years before then.) Don Miguel thought that this wish would be fleeting. But as time passed he was amazed and proud that another desire was fulfilled: his legacy would live on in his daughter.

Maria Dolores stood side by side with her father in her beloved Bar Boadas for more than 30 years, perfecting his techniques and his passion for cocktails.

Spanish novelist Arturo Pérez-Reverte, in his 2000 novel *La Carta Esférica*, best describe the unfaltering popularity of Bar Boadas in the hands of Maria and her husband "Josep":

The woman looked at him curiously. She was smiling a little, perhaps because she was paying attention to the way in which Coy got close to the bar. Instead of staying behind waiting for the bartender to notice him, he moved like a small and compact tow truck among the people that were crowding in front of it. He had ordered a blue gin with tonic for him and a dry martini for her. He brought them back with a skilful pendular like motion of his hands and without spilling a drop. In Boadas, at those hours of the day, that deserved some credit.

A few generations of bartenders have trained at Bar Boadas and continued the family's traditions throughout Barcelona and the rest of Spain. And in recent years, the artistry of Barcelona's bartenders has been discovered around the world—an artistry that carries the Cuban touch with it wherever it goes.

Chapter 10
★ ★ ★ ★

Served with a Smile:
The First -Generation Cantineros

As the Second World War came to a close, Havana experienced a hospitality explosion. Prohibition might have been repealed in the United States, but it did not take any business away from Cuba. Hotels, cabarets, casinos, sprang up not only around the Parque Central, but toward La Rampa. Association graduates earned reputations as stellar as their predecessors, their mentors. The Eden Roc's Elio Moya, Havana Libre's Luis Felipe, El Floridita's Antonio Meilán (creator of the Papa Doble), Tropicana's Celestino González are a minute representation of those who graduated during those early days.

PAPA DOBLE (HEMINGWAY SPECIAL)

2 oz light rum
juice of half a lime
1 teaspoon grapefruit juice
1 teaspoon maraschino
Mix the ingredients in a blender with crushed ice.
Serve without straining in a cocktail glass.

Another graduate, José Maria Váquez created the Mulata.

MULATA

45 ml aged rum
15 ml crème de cacao
15 ml lime juice
Mix the ingredients in a blender with crushed ice.
Serve without straining in a champagne glass.

The association's 490-page, 1948 instruction manual *El Arte de Cantinero*, written by Hilario Alonzo Sanchez, demonstrated the depth of knowledge absorbed by these bar stars.

Even when nationalisation transformed the management of the hospitality industry from one dominated by foreigners to an entirely Cuban owned and operated entity, the cantinero's artistry continued to thrive and evolve. Escuela de Hoteleria was founded, in 1960, at the Gastronomic Union. Two years later, students dressed in white long-sleeved shirts, black trousers and black ties seated themselves in the Aula de Bar room on the second floor of the newly renovated Hotel Sevilla to take their six-month bartending course. A white-smocked Fabio Delgado—who apprenticed in 1936, received his diploma three years later, and presided at Sloppy Joe's—continued the teaching/mentoring legacy that leads to a Barman Class A Diploma.

Today, the Cuban art of employing of a double-jigger, citrus press, mixing glass, shaker, blender, and strainer are second only to a chef-grade comprehension of ingredients from spirits and ice to sugar and spices. These elements combine with the tradition of obsessive detail to presentation and service to create the cantinero's sixth sense—the ultimate expression of the bartender's craft.

Writing, and reading, history is thirsty work. Thankfully, it is time to delve into a few classic Cuban cocktails.

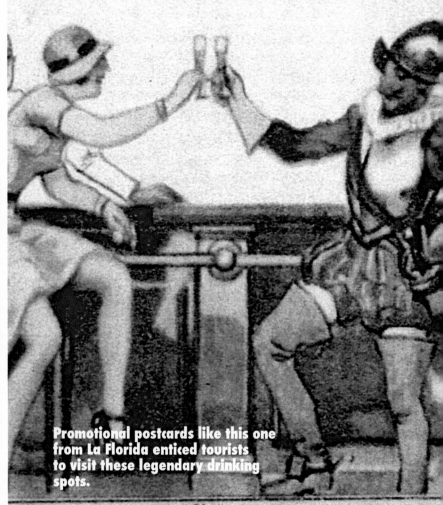

LORIDA
BAR RESTAURANT
THE CRADLE OF THE DAIQUIRI COC

Promotional postcards like this one from La Florida enticed tourists to visit these legendary drinking spots.

RING IN THE "LA FLORIDA

PART TWO ★ ★ ★

A Multi-Coloured Fabric: A History of Cuba's Classic Cocktails

With its long bar and friendly cantineros, Sloppy Joe's was aa favourite destination for military and civilian drinkers.

Chapter 11
★ ★ ★ ★

Introduction

Many classic Cuban cocktails introduced to the American market after Prohibition were imported—especially during the 1940s and 1960s—with histories that were more the inventions of journalists and marketers than the facts. These days it is far easier to research and chronicle who invented a particular recipe or who popularised a given drink. But in the case of Cuban classics, providing a laundry list of names and dates alone would diminish a far more fascinating and realistic truth.

The entirety of the Cuban cocktail repertoire and its golden age is the beverage industry's finest example of how a culture's openness to new ideas and its ability to adapt as well as enhance those concepts makes for a tradition that is wholly unique. What makes Cuban cocktails deserve the honour of being called classics? They have withstood the test of time. Each adapts easily to variation as required by the availability of ingredients and to the regional nature of flavour preference.

In this section we will review the legendary recipes that have deserved this designation.

Chapter 12

Cuba Libre:
From Honey & Rum to Rum & Cola

THE FREEDOM FIGHTERS' DRINK

Cuba Libre. The phrase was most closely associated with the Ten Years' War 1868-1878—not with the Spanish-American War—when the world media first took note of the island nation's fight for independence. But few people realise that it was also linked to a beverage, according to the *New York Herald* newspaper's special commissioner who followed the freedom fighters to the battlefield at Viamones:[43]

> The repast consisted of one dish—roast beef—and nothing else, and in the way of liquids we were invited to hot water, sweetened with honey—a concoction known as "Cuba Libre".

The commissioner had encountered the drink a month earlier when he met up with a "picket guard" of 108 fighters on his way to General Manual Agramonte's headquarters:

> They have meat, with vegetables and oranges and lemons in abundance, but no coffee. Their beverage is hot water, sweetened with honey, which they call Cuba libre. [44]

There are some obvious questions that arise about the ingredients of this Cuba Libre. This newspaperman—as well as others sent to report from the battlefields—was surely relying on translators to aid him in communicating with the revolutionary forces. Therefore it is very difficult to say if this Cuba Libre was

---

43   "CUBA. Report of the Herald Commissioner, Mr. AB Henderson." *New York Herald*, 19 December 1872

44   "INSURGENT CUBA. Herald Special Report from the Seat of Insurrection." New York Herald, 13 November 1872

made with hot water or "burning water" (read: *aguardiente de caña*).

Were the freedom fighters actually drinking rum with honey? Were they drinking Canchánchara, which was later known as the revolutionaries' drink of choice in the jungle?

One other term comes into question. The molasses used to make rum also goes by the same term as honey—*miel*— in Latin American Spanish. So it is hard to say if these American corespondents encountered a hot molasses beverage or a hot honey beverage.

Wouldn't it be ironic if the original Cuba Libre was the Canchánchara, a drink we discuss at length later?

There was a rum and honey beverage that, in 1902, made it into British drinks books that leads one to wonder if this Cuba Libre, this Canchánchara, was exported as Cuban rum took its first steps off the island:

122—RUM AND HONEY. S.D.
Take a wine glass; put in a small piece of ice; and a teaspoonful of Bourbon honey; fill up glass with "Liquid Sunshine" rum; stir well with spoon and place slice of lemon of [SIC] top.[45]

---

45   Paul, Charlie, *Farrow & Jackson Limited's Recipes of American and Other Iced Drinks* (London: Farrow & Jackson Ltd, 1902).

YELLOW JOURNALISM
& THE BIRTH OF A CLICK PHRASE

The phrase "Cuba Libre" was firmly ensconced, by 1898, in the American newspaper vernacular and thus in popular language as evidenced when one US Army post was christened with the name "Camp Cuba Libre":

> Camp Cuba Libre in Jacksonville, Florida, served as the headquarters for the VII Army Corps under the command of General Fitzhugh Lee. Under the General's leadership, Camp Cuba Libre gained a reputation for being one of the better run camps during the war; however, the topography of the campsite led to horrible conditions which made training unbearable and posed many health risks.[46]

American public opinion about Cuba revved up by that point to a fever pitch. Memories of the reports published during the Ten Years' War (1868-1878) were coupled with a constant flow of headlines about the atrocities inflicted by Spanish forces upon Cubans.

Then the mysterious sinking, on 15 February 1898, of the American battleship *USS Maine* in Havana harbour struck the final, tender nerve, especially when newspaper publishers

---

46 http://www.il.ngb.army.mil/Museum/Past/PastSpanishAmerican/
SpanishAmerican.aspx

William Rudolph Hearst and Joseph Pulitzer used the incident as the perfect ploy to increase sales. The outcry to free America's neighbour from Spanish rule—perpetrated by the headlines seen in the *New York Journal* and *The World*—exemplify the power that "yellow journalism" wielded in swaying the public through the use of misleading headlines and sensationalistic reportage, accentuated with lurid illustrations.

Thus, "Cuba Libre!" resounded throughout the US as news syndicates picked up the stories from Bangor ME to San Diego CA. Political pressure then forced the McKinley administration to declare war on Spain. (The Teller Amendment, enacted on 20 April 1898, stipulated that as a result in its involvement in war, the US could not annex Cuba, but had to leave control of the island to its people.)

The Spanish-American War began on 23 April 1898 with its official declaration. The US Navy was sent in to create a sea blockade. Then 300,000 American troops and volunteers, head by General William R Shafter, landed in Daiquirí and Siboney in June to support the approximate 30,000 Cuban freedom fighters.

A little over a month later, the American invasion force pulled up stakes and departed the island. Both Theodore Roosevelt and General Shafter sent requests to President McKinley to leave the island because 75 percent of troops had contracted yellow fever. Evacuation began on 7 August. The US Army left the Ninth Infantry Regiment in place because only 73 of the 984 soldiers had fallen to the disease.[47]

Spain sued for peace after debilitating defeats in Cuba and the Philippines and the fighting ended on 12 August 1898 with the signing of Protocol for Peace. [48] (The final and formal Treaty of Paris was signed on 10 December 1898.[49])

An American flag was raised on Morro Castle in Havana. President McKinley ordered, on New Year's Day 1899, the establishment of a provisional military government headed by General John R Brooke as the conditions of the treaty came into full force on 11 April 1899.

And so ended the passionate association between the phrase "Cuba Libre" and the freedom fighters' beverage.

---

47   Cirillo, Vincent J., Bullets and Bacilli: The Spanish-American War and Military Medicine. (New Brunswick: Rutgers University Press, 2004). This reason this regiment seemed to evade the outbreak was because these volunteers were mostly African-Americans who had been born and raised in the southern US, where yellow fever was common. Thus many of the men had a natural immunity to the disease.

48   The Statutes At Large of the United States of America from March 1897 to March 1899 and Recent Treaties, Conventions, Executive Proclamations, and The Concurrent Resolutions of the Two Houses of Congress, Volume XXX, published by the U.S. Government Printing Office, 1899. Copy courtesy of the U.S. Library of Congress, Asian Division.

49   Healy, David. The United States in Cuba, 1898–1902: Generals, Politicians, and the Search for Policy (Madison: University of Wisconsin Press, 1963).

COCA-COLA ARRIVES IN CUBA

Atlanta drugstore owner and patent medicine manufacturer Asa Griggs Candler had purchased, in 1887, from John Pemberton the formula for the non-alcoholic version of Pemberton's kola nut and coca wine tonic, Coca-Cola. An aggressive marketer, Asa was determined to make his new venture a global enterprise. While the final peace treaty between the US and Spain was still in negotiation, his brother Bishop Warren Candler sailed for Cuba to determine what missionary work could be done there. Being a major stockholder in his brother's company, the bishop also noted in a letter to Asa that:

> We may be sure that commercial currents will follow the channels which education opens and deepens... Here in our duty and our interest coincide.[50]

The wheels were set into motion immediately after the ink dried on the Treaty of Paris and the US took formal possession of Cuba. In May 1899, Asa Candler enlisted wine merchant José Parejo to become the Havana-based wholesaler for Coca-Cola. The product was not

---

50   Pendergrast, Mark. *For God, Country & Coca-Cola: The History of the World's Most Popular Soft Drink (London: The Orion Publishing Group Ltd, 1993 and 2000).*

exported to Cuba until Candler was assured, with American military presence in Cuba, that his investment was safe.

According to the Coca-Cola website:

> In the first two decades of the 20th Century, the international growth of Coca-Cola had been rather haphazard. It began in 1900, when Charles Howard Candler, eldest son of Asa Candler, took a jug of syrup with him on vacation to England. A modest order for five gallons of syrup was mailed back to Atlanta...
> The same year, Coca-Cola travelled to Cuba and Puerto Rico, and it wasn't long before the international distribution of syrup began.[51]

The Anti-Canteen Law that was placed before the US Congress—and eventually passed in 1902— might have helped stimulate interest in the importation of Coca-Cola syrup into Cuba. Alcoholic beverages were not allowed in US Army post exchanges (also known as PXs). So the alleged popularity of the soft drink in Cuba was more than likely based on purchases by the American army personnel not on purchases made by Cuban citizens.[52]

Continued American military presence and an influx of tourism from the US main-

---

51   http://www.thecoca-colacompany.com/heritage/chronicle_man_named_ woodruff.html

52   Littlefield, CE. "Anti-Canteen Legislation and the Army. II", *The North American Review*, Vol. 178, No. 569, pp. 582-596, April 1904.

land boosted sales while Candler expanded his marketing on a global scale. During the 1920s, the Coca-Cola Company assigned the Cuban production operations to its Canadian branch.

THE CUBA LIBRE REAPPEARS —AS A HIGHBALL

There are some historians who have said that the Cuba Libre was invented, in 1902, at La Florida (aka: El Floridita) because of its proximity to the Capitol Building. Why?

Cuban politicians might have celebrated Cuba the election of its first president Tomás Estrada Palma, on 20 May 1902, and its release from American occupation at this favoured venue. But why would La Florida offer a Cuban spirit with an American product to Cubans? The drink does not appear in the 1936 *Bar Florida* book, which provides some evidence that the drink did not originate there.

But this rum-and-cola Cuba Libre does make an appearance in print during the 1920s, painting completely different picture.

HL Mencken, in his 1921 edition of *American Language,* alluded to the fact that in the southern Untied States, people were already mixing Coca-Cola with spirits, especially ones as cheap as Cuban and Puerto Rican rums were prior to Prohibition.

In his 1928 book *When It's Cocktail Time in Cuba*, British playwright and journalist Basil Woon mentioned the presence of this Cuba Libre highball in Havana's American Club:

> Francis Quinlan, his partner. Also a General Motors man. Sometimes plays poker at American Club. Clever at business. Takes his "Cuba Libre" only occasionally."[53]

The American Club, founded in 1902, was a private social club situated at Prado 309, a block from Parque Central. The restaurant, bar, meeting room, and gymnasium were available only to members and their guests. According to the September 1918 edition of *The Rotarian* magazine, the club sported 300 members.

Was it that the bartender at the American Club was responding to the whims of his American customers? Or was it that those club members imported a taste for that drink from other place?

---

53   Woon, Basil. *When It's Cocktail Time in Cuba* (New York: Horace Liveright, 1928). The entry is footnoted: "Cuba Libre: a highball contrived of coca-cola and Bacardí rum."

ON JAMAICAN SHORES

Coca-Cola was a mere import, new to Jamaica when it arrived around 1900. But the company had plenty of native competition that was already well established. Kola wine, kola bitters, kola champagne (which is still produced in Jamaica today as a soft drink) were all being made locally as far back as 1892, when a reporter for *The Daily Gleaner* noted that:

> In homes in different parts of the island the knack of preparing kola as a beverage is understood, and there a cup of kola is at once palatable and refreshing."[54]

A report on an alleged case of fraud appeared in a Kingston, Jamaica newspaper, in November 1899, recorded that the prisoner had come into Andrew Isaacs' tavern and ordered a "drink of Kola and rum which amounted to 6d."[55]

In *The Atlanta Constitution*, the contents of this compound is made clear: Rum was mixed with the popular Jamaican soft drink "kola champagne":

---

54   "The Future of Kola", *The Daily Gleaner*, 23 November 192.

55   "Alleged Forgery Care. Accused Committed." *The Daily Gleaner*, 15 November 1899

He will look forward to the days when he may sit at ease under his luxuriant bread-fruit trees and smoke the pipe of peace and plenty with his favourite beverage, the most delicious drink known to man at his side. Then, under the gentle stimulus of rum and kola champagne, the visions of the great white ships will flit before him—the huge vessels winding up the Port Royal channel in Kingston to show him how he could be protected while taking an important part in the world's work.[56]

This level of popularity naturally sparked interest in commercial production and potential export opportunity. An article about the Jamaican section London's 1905 Crystal Palace exhibition in which two items were proudly displayed:

Messrs McNish Limited show their aerated waters, and certainly nothing in that way could look more beautiful that the Kola Champagne. Lots of people, I hear, have desired to buy the lot but, of course, they are for show during the exhibition. ...The firm of T.M. de Pass of Falmouth, come next with rum and kola "pick-me-up."[57]

56   Haines, Thorton Jenkins, "Uncle Sam's Navy to Maneuver at Kingston, Jamaica to Impress Negroes Who Will Build the Panama Canal," *The Atlanta Constitution*, 23 November 1902.

57   "Jamaica at the Crystal Palace", *The Daily Gleaner*, Kingston Jamaica, 1 July 1905.

The company wasn't the only one to produce a packaged rum and kola beverage. An advertisement appearing in the 3 February 1912 edition of *The Daily Gleaner* demonstrates the strong interest and popularity of the compound made with Jamaican rum:

Rum and Kola appeared more prominently in the advertisement that appeared in *The Daily Gleaner*'s 6 December 1909 edition:

EVERY ONE
CANNOT DO BETTER THAN DRINK
Rum and Kola
As bottled (together) by the
Popular Aerated Water Co
PORT ANTONIO,
In pint bottles at 2s per dozen net
In Splits at 3s 6d per dozen
This drink has the nutty flavour of the K
blended with Jamaica's Pure Rum.
We are the Sole Manufacturers

Rum and cola made its first appearance in fiction in a 1908 novel in which the hero orders a "Highball" in Kingston, Jamaica:

Well, he would do almost anything except eat bananas. He walked swiftly to the town and stopped only long enough to drink three high-balls of rum and cola. Ah, the sparkling cola ! He must have that. Then he took the train for Kingston. "The Enos is lying at the dock at Port Antonio," said Mr. Booker, after he had greeted his man coldly and formally. " You will proceed there and take command. Go down at once and see Johns. He'll give you your examination at once. Get your ticket and go. Then wait for further orders. James will be mate." McDuff grinned. " Ah, weel, I ken he'll be a noddy wan — ah, man, man, but I'll fair dress him down into shape," he said, shifting his watery gaze over the room. " You can dress him all you want," said Mr. Booker. [58]

This story leads to the believe that the taste for rum and Kola Champagne inspired experimentation with rum and Coca-Cola amongst Corps of Army Engineer officers and other members of the American armed forces who encountered the drink in Jamaica.

Americans had thoroughly embraced Highballs during the late 1800s, especially the Rickey.

A RICKEY BY ANY OTHER NAME

The tales goes that the Rickey was born, in 1883, at Shoomaker's Bar in Washington DC by barman George A Williamson in collaboration with US Democratic lobbyist Colonel Joe Rickey. A compound made from bourbon, soda water, and lime, US Representative William Henry Hatch and Fred Mussey were present at its birth and came in regularly to ask for a "Joe Rickey drink" or say "I'll have a Joe Rickey."[59]

---

58   Haines, Thorton Jenkins, *Bahama Bill: Mate of the Wrecking Sloop Sea-Horse* (Boston: LC Page & Company, 1908)

59   Brown, George Rothwell. *Washington: A Not Too Serious History* (Baltimore: The Norman Publishing Company, 1930).

JOE RICKEY

2 oz bourbon
Half of a lime squeezed and dropped into the glass
Soda water
Put bourbon, lime and shell in a highball or wine
glass. Add ice, stir. Then fill with soda water.

A decade later, the drink morphed into the Gin Rickey which topped the charts in bars across the country after it first appeared at the 1893 Columbian Exposition in Chicago.[60]

GIN RICKEY

2 oz gin
Half of a lime squeezed and dropped into the glass
Soda water
Put gin, lime and shell in a highball or wine glass.
Add ice, stir. Then fill with soda water.

The Gin Rickey trumped the popularity of the Mamie Taylor—a Scotch highball made with ginger beer and lime—between the 1890s and the dawn of Prohibition.

Both drinks and their origins made for colourful reading in newspapers across the United States. And judging by Mencken's remark about Americans mixing cola soda with spirits before Prohibition it is quite possible that

60   Brown, George Rothwell. *Washington: A Not Too Serious History* (Baltimore: The Norman Publishing Company, 1930).

both Jamaican and American cultural influences played a strong role in birth of the Cuba Libre.

A TRAGIC DIGRESSION

At the height of Prohibition, Americans who could not afford to make their way to Cuba to have a drink resorted to numerous alternatives. One of the saddest cases was the imbibing of Jamaican Ginger Extract which was known as "Jake". An early patent medicine, Jake contained 70-80 percent ABV and in of itself was not dangerous. However, the US Treasury Department, noting that Jake had to potential of crossing Prohibition laws required that manufacturers had to add at least 5 grams of ginger solids per cubic centimetre of alcohol. This made Jake difficult to drink.

Some bootleggers simply replaced the ginger solids with a small amount of ginger and either castor oil or molasses to pass inspection. But bootleggers Harry Gross and Max Reisman found their way around the ruling by using a plasticizer called tri-o-tolyl phosphate (TOCP) instead of ginger solids. It passed the government tests and was more palatable to consumers.

But there was a hitch. TOCP contained a neurotoxin that caused damage to the nervous system In 1930, large numbers of Jake drinkers lost control of their extremities. Some were paralysed. The terms "jake walk," "jake leg," and "jake paralysis" entered the public consciousness. Within a few months the adulterated Jake was taken off the market.

This did not help the estimated 30,000 to 50,000 victims who were afflicted, many of whom were recent immigrants and even more who were poor or poverty-stricken.

Why do we mention this catastrophe?

Because Coca-Cola mixed with Jake was a popular way to consume this lethal liquid. An article in 1927 edition of *The Outlook* bears witness to this:

He did report a few disquieting minor discoveries. Hip flasks were for sale in Kansas cigar stores. Forty thousand gallons of Jamaica ginger were shipped into Texas in 1924-5; the normal consumption is estimated at about three hundred gallons. (I am told that Coca Cola fortified with Jamaica ginger makes a drink with a powerful kick.) In Oklahoma he saw the can of malt with the familiar legend telling the customer what not to do—or fermentation will take place. But trustworthy studies on a scale that would show a relation between the Eighteenth Amendment and bank deposits, or crime, or public health, were not available. "Well," I said, "suppose you had come back with a car-load of prime figures. What then? What have bank clearances to do with this issue?" I was serious; but he seemed to sense flippancy and refused to argue.[61]

Even the poorest person in America still had a taste for spirits—in any form they could acquire—and Coca-Cola at the height of Prohibition.

THE CUBA LIBRE LANDS IN THE US

Let's start by saying that the Cuba Libre was not the only drink made of rum, lime, and Coca-Cola. A few versions were promoted during the 1930s.

The Puerto Rico Distilling Company marketed its own version—the Carioca Cooler—lauding it as the "Smartest Summer Drink" in the 3 August 1935 edition of *The New Yorker*.

CARIOCA COOLER

1 jigger Rum Carioca
1/2 Lemon or Lime
Coca-Cola [62]

---

61   Abbott, Ernest Hamlin, Abbott, Lyman, Bellany, Francis Rufus, Mabie, Hamilton Wright. *The Outlook: An Illustrated Weekly of Current Life*, Volume 147 (New York: Outlook Co, 1927).

62   "Smartest Summer Drink", *The New Yorker*, 3 August 1935.

Coasters such as this one, further marketed the drink:

The 1935 print campaign was quite extensive when it was launched. Notice the progression of advertisements copyrighted by American Spirits that summer as recorded in the 1935 *Catalog of Copyright Entries, Part 1, Books, Group 2, Volume 32*:

— Carioca is continental, rum Carioca ©June 1, 1935

— Did it start in Hollywood? ©June 27, 1935

— Don't say rum—say Carioca ©June 4, 1935

— Drink at the Astor, rum Carioca ©June 25, 1935

— Drink at the Paradise, rum Carioca ©June 18, 1935

— Drink at the Waldorf, rum Carioca ©June 12, 1935

— New rum drink becomes famous overnight ©May 30, June 20, 1935

— There's Rio in Carioca, rum Carioca © June 1, 1935

— There's romance in rum, rum Carioca © June 1, 1935

— Wanted. Name of bon vivant who discovered new rum drink! © June 6, 1935

— Who discovered the Carioca Cooler? ©June 13, 1935

— Yo-ho-ho, rum Carioca © June 1, 1935

This Carioca Cooler campaign was spearheaded by Walter Ruby, who acted as advertising manager of the American Spirits Company between 1935 and 1936. And then, a year later, the Carioca Cooler made the news in New York:

Present plans call for intensive promotion of the Carioca; the West Indies, electrically mixed daiquiri, and the Carioca Cooler.[63]

It must have been a very effective promotion, given its national distribution. But it also seems to have caused a good deal of controversy. An item that appeared first in the 1940 *Court of Customs and Patent Appeals, Volume 28* noted that:

63   "Rum Campaign Starts Here," *The New York Times*, 21 July 1937.

You will note an interesting article in connection with
the first Fall meeting of the IBA, which meeting was
addressed by a well-known wine and liquor authority,
Mr G Selmer Fougner.

This article leaves no doubt that the Carioca Rum Company is very closely associated with the Coca Cola Company in the promotion of a drink known as the Carioca Cooler. The presence of Mr. Homer Thompson of the New York Coca- Cola Bottling Company, at this meeting, is further indicative of the association.

Naturally, the writer is at quite a loss to understand your statement to him at the time of our meeting several months ago, at which you stated definitely that the Coca-Cola Company had no association whatsoever with the Carioca Rum Company and, as a matter of fact, had secured an injunction against these people for the use of the Coca-Cola name and facsimile of the bottle in their advertising.

Appellee's attorneys, in replying to said letter, denied the association with the Carioca Rum Company referred to in the letter, but attention is called to it here for the reason that, if appellant's selling agent believed that appellee was interested in a beverage containing rum, it is altogether likely that purchasers of appellant's goods bearing the mark ...[64]

---

64   *Court of Customs and Patent Appeals*, Volume 28, (Untied States Court of Customs and Patent Appeals, 1940) p 1153.

Either the Coca Cola Company decided to abandon a relationship with the American Spirits Company or never had one. But the campaign disappeared from circulation by the time Lord Invader's (aka: Rupert Grant) and Lionel Belasco's song "Rum and Coca Cola" was a huge hit on the 1945 US pop singles charts.

Recorded by the Andrews Sisters with lyrics that had been reworked by entertainer Morey Amsterdam, the tune brought both Rum & Cola-Cola as well as Cuba Libre to the American public.

VARIATIONS ABOUND

A & G J Caldwell, Inc, producers of a New England rum since 1790 called Caldwell's Rum, marketed what they called "The Better Cuba Libre" in their 1939 promotional pamphlet.

Dubbed Caldwell's Rum Cola, one of the last New England rum producers tried desperately to capitalise on the post-Prohibition push to revive the American rum market.

CALDWELL'S RUM COLA

Make in Highball Glass
1 jigger Caldwell's Old Newburyport Rum
Juice of half a Lime, put peel in glass

Add ice and fill with any of the cola beverages For a taller drink, use a Collins glass and 2 oz of Old Newburyport Rum.

Another Cuba Libre recipe of a completely different make and model authored by L M Lawson appeared, in 1935, in the *El Paso Herald-Post*:[65]

CUBA LIBRE (LM LAWSON VERSION)

1/3 Bacardí rum
1/3 gin
1/3 lime juice
A little grenadine [66]

Author Sydney Clark alluded to the fact that Cuba Libres had made it to Miami in his 1936 novel *Cuban Tapestry*:

Cuba Libre seemed to be the drink in vogue in the Miami and we all ordered it. ...The " Free Cuba" is merely Coca-Cola flavored to taste with Bacardí.[67]

---

65   Luther, Betty, "Try Cuba Libre Before Eating Edwards Chicken", *El Paso Daily Herald-Post*, 11 July 1935.

66   Luther, Betty, "Try Cuba Libre Before Eating Edwards Chicken", *El Paso Daily Herald-Post*, 11 July 1935.

67   Clark, Sydney. *Cuban Tapestry* (New York: RM McBride & Company, 1936).

By this time, the free bar at the Bacardí Building in Havana had courted American journalists, writers, and celebrities for five years.

Cuba Libre had made it into the American mainstream. In 1939, Charles H Baker Jr described the Cuba Libre by saying that:

> This native Island concoction started by accident and has caught on everywhere throughout the south, has filtered through the north and west. Last summer, for instance, we ran into Kooba Lee-brays 5000 feet up in the North Carolina Mountains at High Hampton, the year before in Mexico City and Seattle. Last week in Palm Beach and Cat Cay. The only trouble with the drink is that it started by accident and without imagination, has been carried along by the ease of its supply. Under any condition it is too sweet.[68]

His solution came as a result of experimentation:

> What's to do?...After clinical experimenting for which our insurance carriers heartily dislike us, we tested several variations of the original with this result: The Improved Cuba Libre consists of 1 big jigger of Carta de Oro Bacardí, the juice of a 1 small green lime, and the lime peel after squeezing. Put in a Tom Collins glass, muddle well to get oil worked up over the sides

---

68   Baker, Charles H, Jr, *The Gentleman's Companion: Volume II, Being an Exotic Drinking Book or, Around the Word with Jigger, Beaker and Flask* (New York: Derrydale Press, 1939).

of the glass, add lots of ice lumps, and fill up with a
bottle of chilled coca cola. Stir up once, and salud y
pesetas![69]

Albert Stevens Crockett devoted an
entire chapter to Cuban cocktail in his 1935
book *The Old Waldorf-Astoria Bar Book*, which
he prefaced by noting that:

From Will P Taylor, manager of the Hotel National in
Havana, who stuck at his post all through the recent
local disturbances, which included a bombardment
of his hotel, I have obtained the choicest Cuban Rum
recipes.[70]

CUBA LIBRE (CROCKETT VERSION)

Half portions of Bacardí and Coca Cola

Who was Albert Stevens Crockett?
He was another American journalist
who fancied himself an authority on mixed
drinks. Fellow journalist and drink book author
Lawrence Blochman described Crockett thus:

---

69   Baker, Charles H, Jr, *The Gentleman's Companion: Volume II, Being an Exotic Drinking Book or, Around the Word with Jigger, Beaker and Flask* (New York: Derrydale Press, 1939).

70   Crockett, Albert Stevens, " *The Old Waldorf-Astoria Bar Book* (New York: AS Crockett, 1935).

Albert Stevens Crockett, doyen of the Overseas Press Club, has been many things in his long career, including the first American correspondent to tour Europe by automobile back in 1904.[71]

In Blochman's 1957 book, a Cuba Libre is prescribed in a more generic fashion that the one found in Crockett's chronicle of the old Waldorf-Astoria:

CUBA LIBRE (BLOCHMAN VERSION)

1 jigger Cuban rum
1/2 lime (juice and peel)
Bottled cola
Put the lime and rum in a 10-ounce glass with a few ice cubes and fill with cola. Stir gently.[72]

The drink appears in attorney David Embury's 1947 book without making any distinction between a Cuba Libre and a Rum and Coca-Cola:

---

71   Blochman, Lawrence, *A Round the World Bar Guide: Here's How: Nearly 400 Drink Recipes, from America's Most Famous Foreign Correspondents – Members of the Overseas Press Club* (New York: Signet, 1957).

72   Blochman, Lawrence, *A Round the World Bar Guide: Here's How: Nearly 400 Drink Recipes, from America's Most Famous Foreign Correspondents – Members of the Overseas Press Club* (New York: Signet, 1957).

CUBA LIBRA
OR RUM AND COCA-COLA (EMBURY VERSION)

Juice of 1 small lime (drop in 1/2 lime shell, too)

2 ounces White Label Rum

Put ingredients in collins glass, add 3 or 4 large ice cubes, fill up with Coca-Cola, stir quickly and serve.[73]

Vic Begeron's 1947 *Bartender's Guide... by Trader Vic* included a Cuba Libre. (However, his 1946 *Trader Vic's Food & Drink* does not.) But what is more interesting is that Bergeron also crafted a Cuba Libre Cocktail recipe with an amazingly different profile.

CUBA LIBRE (TRADER VIC VERSION)

1 green lime

2 oz Bacardí

Coca-Cola

Cut lime and squeeze into Tom Collins glass, dropping shells; muddle the lime shells and add cracked ice and rum. Stir and fill glass with Coca-Cola.[74]

---

73   Embury, David Augustus, *The Fine Art of Mixing Drinks* (New York: Doubleday, 1948).

74   Bergeron, Victor Jules, *Bartender's Guide...by Trader Vic* (Garden City: Doubleday, 1947).

CUBA LIBRE COCKTAIL
(TRADER VIC VERSION)

1 oz Cuban rum
1 oz Coca-Cola
Juice 1/2 lime
Shake with cracked ice; strain into cocktail glass.[75]

In American journalist and author Lucius Beebe's 1946 *The Stork Club Bar Book*, not only was a Cuba Libre recipe present, he provided the key as to why Cuban drinks had become popular calls saying that advertising and promotion couples with aggressively cheap pricing were the primary causes for Cuban rum's success stateside.

The third factor was the "feminine factor in public drinking, since it is universally acknowledged that the thin consistency combined with special suitability of Cuban type rums for mixing with fruits and sugar have a strong appeal to women's taste."

Beebe then cited "the shrewd approach which was made by the manufacturers and distributors of pale rums through the agency of snob appeal and name publicization." He contined with his own "celebrity" first encounter with the drink.

---

75   Bergeron, Victor Jules, *Bartender's Guide...by Trader Vic* (Garden City: Doubleday, 1947).

The first Cuba Libre the author ever encountered
was being drunk by George Jean Nathan in the
super-elegant purlieus of the Colony Restaurant and
it was from such beginnings as this that the Frozen
Daiquirí became as familiar a household property in
Social Circle, Georgia, and Fort Madison, Iowa, as the
Hoover vacuum cleaner.[76]

Beebe made his point. George Jean Nathan was a famed American drama critic and editor who rubbed elbows with the celebrity set just as Beebe and Walter Winchell did at famed Stork Club's back VIP room. Often called the world's most expensive restaurant during the 1940s, the Colony Restaurant, located at 667 Madison Avenue at 61st Street, boasted a regular roster of a-listers from Frank Sinatra to the Duke and Duchess of Windsor to Aristotle Onassis. The restaurant was also where the city's most famed restaurateur, Sirio Maccioni of Le Cirque, learnt his trade in hospitality as The Colony's maitre d' during the 1960s.

Until it closed its doors in 1965, The Stork Club (3 East 53rd Street, near Fifth Avenue), served its Cuba Libre in the following manner:

---

76   Beebe, Lucius. *The Stork Club Bar Book* (New York: Rinehart & Company, Inc, 1946).

CUBA LIBRE (STORK CLUB VERSION)

2 oz rum
Insert juice of half lime and rind in tall glass
2 cubes ice
Fill with Coca Cola. Stir.[77]

> Riled that a civilian the likes of attorney David Embury had the audacity to write a best-selling cocktail book, *The Fine Art of Mixing Drinks*, Jack Townsend—head bartender at Manhattan's famed 21 Club—wrote his own volume in 1951, *The Bartender's Book*, in which he summed up the Cuba Libre's rise in popularity:

> The Cuba Libre was made famous by a wartime Calypso song, extolling the virtues of the Yankee dollah, a recording of which hit very juke box in the Western Hemisphere. It was dinned into bartenders' ears to such an extent that they developed a mild allergy even to the drink. Long before the Trinidad Calypso singers took up its praise, however, Carioca rum was being combined with Coca Cola to make the Cuba Libre a sophisticated drink. The critic George Jean Nathan was one of the first to be seen drinking the mixture at the Colony [Restaurant]. The Cuba Libre seems to be gaining in popularity, probably because of its extreme simplicity. It is the drink of the younger set. Our popularity poll discloses that women order it oftener than men do, but there is no indication that men bypass it to any extent. As long as both

77   Beebe, Lucius. *The Stork Club Bar Book* (New York: Rinehart & Company, Inc, 1946).

products are sold and people have a taste for long sweetish drinks, the Cuba Libre probably will lead the rum list.[78]

CUBA LIBRE (TOWNSEND VERSION)

1 1/2 oz rum
Coca Cola
Juice and rind of half lime
Squeeze lime juice into 12-oz glass. Drop in rind.
Add ice cubs and Coca Cola and stir.[79]

No word was mentioned during the 1940s and 1950s of an American military person inventing the drink as happened by the 1960s, thanks to Fausto Rodriguez and Bacardi's ad campaign.

In fact, a 1968 book that documented famous drinks created by American armed forces titled *Cups of Valour* does not contain a recipe for a Cuba Libre even though it does have the formulae for Jungle Juice, Gannasanna, and the ubiquitous French 75.

Before its recent advertising campaign, which claims that the Cuba Libre was invented in 1900 at an American Bar in Old Havana, Bacardí originally stated that:

78   Townsend, Jack and McBride, Tom Moore, *The Bartender's Book* (New York: Penguin Group, 1951).

79   Townsend, Jack and McBride, Tom Moore, *The Bartender's Book* (New York: Penguin Group, 1951).

One afternoon, a group of off-duty soldiers from the U.S. Signal Corps were gathered in a bar in Old Havana. Fausto Rodriguez, a young messenger, later recalled that Captain Russell came in and ordered Bacardí (Gold) rum and Coca-Cola on ice with a wedge of lime. The captain drank the concoction with such pleasure that it sparked the interest of the soldiers around him. They had the bartender prepare a round of the captain's drink for them. ...When they ordered another round, one soldier suggested that they toast ¡Por Cuba Libre! in celebration of the newly freed Cuba.[80]

What was the source of this marketing campaign?

A 1966 Bacardí advertisement that ran in *Life* magazine featured two men dressed in US military uniforms plus a third man who are sitting around table with a modern-day Coke bottle and a bottle of rum. The headline read: "So that's how 'Rum & Coke' was invented!"[81]

A very legal-looking affidavit filled the rest of the page.

---

80   "Cuba Libre" http://en.wikipedia.org/wiki/Cuba_Libre#cite_note-cuba-libre-1

81   http://www.cigaraficionado.com/webfeatures/show/id/7600/p/1

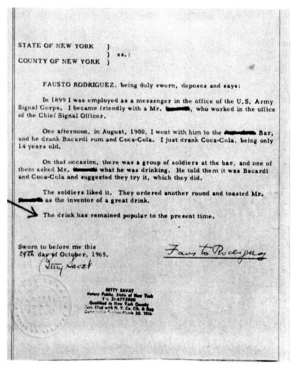

STATE OF NEW YORK)
) ss.:
COUNTY OF NEW YORK)

FAUSTO RODRIGUEZ, being duly sworn, deposes and says:

In 1899 I was employed as a messenger in the office of the U.S. Army Signal Corps. I became friendly with a Mr. ▬▬▬, who worked in the office of the Chief Signal Officer.

One afternoon, in August, 1900, I went with him to the ▬▬▬ Bar, and he drank Bacardi rum and Coca-Cola. I just drank Coca-Cola, being only 14 years old.

On that occasion, there was a group of soldiers at the bar, and one of them asked Mr. ▬▬▬ what he was drinking. He told them it was Bacardi and Coca-Cola and suggested they try it, which they did.

The soldiers liked it. They ordered another round and toasted Mr. ▬▬▬ as the inventor of a great drink.

The drink has remained popular to the present time.

Sworn to before me this
24th day of October, 1965.

Fausto Rodriguez

Betty Savat

BETTY SAVAT
Notary Public, State of New York
31-5772900
Qualified in New York County
Cert. filed with N. Y. Co. Clk. & Reg.
Commission Expires March 30, 1966

The ad appeared on the heels of the 1965 "Things Go Better with Coke" campaign and after a joint marketing venture was signed off by Bacardí's National Sales Promotion Manager, Fausto Rodriguez.[82]

There is not a trace of evidence that an American Bar or a Bar Americano ever existed on Calle Neptuno. But there is more information available about Fausto Rodriguez.

82   http://www.cigaraficionado.com/webfeatures/show/id/7600/p/1

WHO WAS FAUSTO RODRIGUEZ?

Born in Santa Clara, Cuba on 16 July 1886, Rodriguez arrived in Miami FL on 9 March 1928 on the vessel *Evangeline* from Havana. He declared his intention to become a US citizen in 1935 and was married in new York City on 14 September 1936 to an American woman from Philadelphia named Helaine.[83]

According to his 1937 Petition for Naturalisation, he had moved up in the world, residing at the Barbizon-Plaza Hotel at 58th and Sixth Avenue, which during the 1930s was a fashionable mode of habitation. His witnesses were Francis A O'Neill, an attorney, and William A Dalton, a New York Telephone executive and President of the prestigious New York Athletic Club.[84]

(It is interesting to note that the Barbizon-Plaza Hotel where Rodriguez resided played a significant role in Cuban cocktail history. It is the same establishment that was named in the Bacardí Cocktail lawsuit that was

---

83   United States of America Petition for Naturalization No. 28768 dated 29 January 1937.

84   United States of America Petition for Naturalization No. 28768 dated 29 January 1937.

filed by the Bacardí company in 1936. This matter will discussed later in this chapter.)[85]

Rodriguez was appointed, in July 1952, by Bacardí Imports, New York, as the company's national sales promotion manager. This was not his first position with Bacardí. Previously he was manager of the company's hotel and club division.[86]

The year after Fausto Rodriguez signed the affidavit that was used in the Bacardí Cuba Libre print ad campaign, died in September 1966 in New York.[87] And the use of the term "Cuba Libre" for this rum and cola drink disappeared from Bacardí's promotional materials.

1976 and 1979 when they published The Bacardí Party Book pamphlet:

BACARDÍ & COLA

Pour a jigger or two of Bacardí light over ice cubes in a tall glass. Fill with your favorite cola (or diet cola). Squeeze and drop in a lemon or lime wedge.[88]

---

85   This was also a period in Bacardí's history when it was fighting for the right to produce its rum in Puerto Rico to escape the new American tariffs on imported spirits. Establishing Bacardí production in the American Territory of Puerto Rico meant the company had a major marketing advantage in the US.("Curbs Rum Manufacture: Puerto Rican Law Bars Outsiders—Modification May Be Sought", *The New York Times*, 26 May 1936. "Bacardi Runs Puerto Rico Plant", *The New York Times*, 18 April 1937. "Puerto Rico Bacardi Firms Wins in high Court; Hughes Declares Trade-Mark Ban Is Invalid," *The New York Times*, 10 December 1940.)

86   "Advertising and Marketing News", *The New York Times*, 9 July 1952.

87   Social Security Death Index, SSN: 091-01-0670.

88   "The Bacardi Party Book," 1976 and 1979.

CONCLUSIONS
ABOUT THE CUBA LIBRE

Prior to the 1898 Spanish-American War, there was a drink consumed by Cuban freedom fighters that was called a Cuba Libre in the American press. But it did not contain a cola drink.

The Cuba Libre does not appear in any Cuban cocktail book that was published between the 1900s through 1950s including the 1927 *El Arte de Hacer un Cocktail y Algo Más* and the 1948 *El Arte del Cantineros*.

Although it is mentioned as a drink consumed in 1928 by an American executive who was a member of the American Club in Havana, the rum-and-cola Cuba Libre does not make an appearance in print until 1935 in the US.

It appears that lime juice became a standard in the recipe after the 1930s promotional campaign for the Carioca Cooler brought it to prominence.

Although some sources make the distinction between Cuba Libre and Rum & Coca-Cola by citing the inclusion of lime in the former, there is no basis that this is the truth. In fact, based on David Embury's 1947 recipe, the two drinks were one in the same.

A CHRONOLOGICAL TABLE OF CUBA LIBRE RECIPES

YEAR	SOURCE	DRINK NAME	RECIPE
1872	New York Herald	Cuba Libre	"hot water" sweetened with honey
1902	Farrow & Jackson Limited's Recipes for American and Other Iced Drinks	Rum and Honey	Take a wine glass; put in a small piece of ice; and a teaspoonful of Bourbon honey; fill up glass with "Liquid Sunshine" rum; stir well with spoon and place slice of lemon of [SIC] top.
1928	When It's Cocktail Time in Cuba	Cuba Libre	Cuba Libre: a highball contrived of coca-cola and Bacardí rum.
1935	The New Yorker	Carioca Cooler	1 jigger Rum Carioca 1/2 Lemon or Lime Coca-Cola
1935	El Paso Herald-Post	LM Lawson's Cuba Libre	1/3 Bacardí rum 1/3 gin 1/3 lime juice a little grenadine
1935	The Old Waldorf-Astoria Bar Book	Cuba Libre	Half portions of Bacardí and Coca Cola

YEAR	SOURCE	DRINK NAME	RECIPE
1939	The Gentleman's Companion: An Exotic Drink Book	Improved Cuba Libre	1 big jigger of Carta de Oro Bacardí, the juice of a 1 small green lime, and the lime peel after squeezing. Put in a Tom Collins glass, muddle well to get oil worked up over the sides of the glass, add lots of ice lumps, and fill up with a bottle of chilled coca cola
1939	Here's How: Caldwell's Rum pamphlet	Caldwell's Rum Cola	Make in Highball Glass 1 jigger Caldwell's Old Newburyport Rum Juice of half a Lime, put peel in glass Add ice and fill with any of the cola beverages For a taller drink, use a Collins glass and 2 oz of Old Newburyport Rum.
1946	The Stork Club Bar Book	Cuba Libre	2 oz rum insert juice of half lime and rind in tall glass 2 cubes ice Fill with Coca Cola Stir.

YEAR	SOURCE	DRINK NAME	RECIPE
1947	The Fine Art of Mixing Drinks	Cuba Libre or Rum & Coca-Cola	Juice of 1 small lime (drop in 1/2 lime shell, too) 2 ounces White Label Rum Put ingredients in collins glass, add 3 or 4 large ice cubes, fill up with Coca-Cola, stir quickly and serve.
1948	Trader Vic's Bartender's Guide	Cuba Libre	1 green lime 2 oz Bacardí Coca-Cola Cut lime and squeeze into Tom Collins glass, dropping shells; muddle the lime shells and add cracked ice and rum. Stir and fill glass with Coca-Cola.
1948	Trader Vic's Bartender's Guide	Cuba Libre Cocktail	1 oz Cuban rum 1 oz Coca-Cola Juice 1/2 lime Shake with cracked ice; strain into chilled cocktail glass.
1951	The Bartender's Book	Cuba Libre	1 1/2 oz Carioca rum Coca Cola juice and rind of half lime Squeeze lime juice into 12-oz glass. Drop in rind. Add ice cubs and Coca Cola and stir.

YEAR	SOURCE	DRINK NAME	RECIPE
1957	Here's How	Cuba Libre	1 jigger Cuban rum 1/2 lime (juice and peel) Bottled cola Put the lime and rum in a 10-ounce glass with a few ice cubes and fill with cola. Stir gently.
1965	Advertisement with Fausto Rodrigeuz deposition	Cuba Libre	Bacardí and Coca-Cola (no proportions provided)
1976 and 1979	The Bacardí Party Book	Bacardí & Cola	Pour a jigger or two of Bacardí light over ice cubes in a tall glass. Fill with your favorite cola (or diet cola). Squeeze and drop in a lemon or lime wedge.

Even when Prohibition was repealed, American tourists flocked by the thousands to Havana's bars.

Chapter 13

The Daiquirí:
An Identity Crisis

PONCHE: THE BRITISH DRINK

The essential Rum Sour, the Daiquirí, is our next exploration. We begin this story by going back to an overwhelmingly popular beverage that ruled the drinks menu for over 200 years—punch.

In a 1760 French translation of the 1743 proceedings of the Royal Society of London, Punch—or "the Perfect Fifth"—is described as containing water, sugar, lemon, and eau-de-vie. But for use in the autumn and winter, one should eliminate the lemon and increase the sugar and spirit:

Le Ponche, ou le Diapente, comme je l'ai appelle improprement, je fait ansi: Prenez deux livres d'eau, une once & demie de sucre, deux onces & demie de juc [sic] de limon récent, trois onces & demie d'eau de vie, mêlez le tout ensemble. C'est le ponche que nous bûvons communément en Eté; mais celui dont nous faison usage en Automne & en Hiver est plus fort, contenant plus de sucre & d'eau de vie, & moins d'acide. C'est une boisson agréable, acidule & rafraîchissante; elle fait un excellent diaphorétique dans le temps chaud & un bon diurétique dans un temps froid.[89]

PONCHE OR DIAPENTE

16 ounces water
1 ½ ounces sugar
2 ½ ounces fresh lemon juice
3 ½ ounces spirit

Sounds familiar, doesn't it?

---

89 *Transactions Philosophiques de la Société Royale de Londres pour le Mois de Février 1743*, No. 470, Volume 7 (Paris: Chez Piget, 1760).

In his 1734 dictionary of French, Spanish, and Latin, author Francisco Sobrino defined *ponche* as a British drink made from *aguardiente*, water, lemon, and sugar.

PONCHE, s.s. Ponche, bebida Inglesa, que le hace de aguardiente, agua, limon y azucar. [90]

Is it possible that the British introduced Punch to Cuba?

British East India Company seamen, freebooters, and adventurers travelling the Indian Ocean in the early 1600s quickly adopted Punch (derived from *panch*, the Hindi term for the number "five"). Made from five ingredients: sugar, lemon, water, tea, and arrack, this libation lured the sipper with the exotic tastes of citrus, sugar, and tea that they had otherwise not experienced in seventeenth-century Europe.

It is likely that the citrus juice coupled with the addictive sweetness of sugar made this drink irresistible to scurvy-prone, vitamin-C-deficient sailors.

In the West Indies, one would be pretty hard pressed to find a local source for tea. Already popular at home, it was no surprise that seamen crafted a rum version. Captain William Dampier mentioned how widespread this

90   Sobrino, Francisco. *Nouveau Dictionnaire de Sobrino, François, Espangol et Latin*, Tome III, p. 381 (Bruxelles, 1734).

"punch" was in his 1699 memoirs, commenting that while he was on the island of Tortuga he noticed that:

> Ships coming from some of the Caribbean islands are always well stored with Rum, Sugar, and Lime-juice to make Punch, to hearten their Men when they are at work getting and bringing aboard the Salt; and they commonly provide the more, in hopes to meet with Privateers, who resort hither in the aforesaid Months, purposely to keep a Christmas, as they call it, being sure to meet with Liquor enough to be merry with, and are very liberal to those that treat them.[91]

THE BRITISH INFLUENCE ON THE CUBAN PALATE

The tradition of providing regular seamen with a daily tot of rum had long been established within the British Royal Navy.

In 1655, vice-Admiral William Penn (later to become the founder of Pennsylvania) arrived in Barbados and captured Jamaica during his campaign to claim the West Indies on behalf of Britain's head of state Oliver Cromwell. During the long ocean voyage, the daily

91   Dampier, Captain William, *A New Voyage Round the World* (London: James Knapton, 1699).

beer and wine rations ran out and the French brandy given to officers was frowned upon: a casualty from the Thirty Years War, when French and German products were generally banned in Britain.

Rum was plentiful. Rum was cheap. Rum was familiar to the sailors who had encountered cachaça (*aguardiente*) since Elizabethan times. It gave Penn the perfect reason to initiate the rum ration amongst the fleet sailing the Caribbean. Other fleets adopted the same practice. Rum was decreed, by 1687, an official part of sailors' daily rations. In 1731,the gallon of beer ration was completely replaced with a half pint of 140-170 proof rum (equivalent to a pint of 80 proof) in "Regulations and Instructions Relating to his Majesty's Service at Sea." It was a practice that continued until the 1970s.

The British Royal Navy's vice-Admiral Edward Vernon (nicknamed Old Grog because of his waterproof grogam coat made from gum-stiffened silk, wool, and mohair that he wore on deck) issued an order on 21 August 1740 that the daily rum ration should be: "…every day mixed with the proportion of a quart of water to a half pint of rum, to be mixed in a scuttled butt kept for that purpose, and to be done upon the deck, and in the presence of the Lieutenant of the Watch who is to take particular care to see that the men are not defrauded in having their full allowance of rum…and let those that are good husband men receive extra lime juice and sugar that to be made more palatable to them."

During the Seven Years' War (1754-1763) the British Royal Navy captured the Spanish colonial city of Havana in the 1762 Battle of Havana that lasted from March through August. The city was not returned to the Spanish crown until 1763 with the signing of the Treaty of Paris. This would have been enough time for a certain amount of British influence to enter the Cuban cultural fabric.

With the obvious availability of *aguardiente de caña* in Cuba, the fleet took advantage of the local supply.

But there is also evidence of a local concoction made from the same or similar ingredients.

CANCHÁNCHARA: A CUBAN ORIGINAL

Canchánchara— a simple compound of honey, aguardiente and lemon juice—is believed by some historians to have been invented during the Ten Years War (1868-1878) in Trinidad, Cuba. Others say that it was born in the eastern part of the island.

CANCHÁNCHARA

60 ml aguardiente
2 spoonfuls honey
1 teaspoon lemon juice
Ice
Mix well in a glass the honey and lime juice. Add
aguardiente and ice. Stir.[92]

During the 1800s the drink may not have necessarily been made with rum, but with *aguardiente de caña*, which was cheaper and equally abundant in Cuba. But was honey the original sweetener? *Miel*—being another term for the molasses used in rum production—could be just that. Molasses, not honey.

Yet the 1872 *New York Herald* special commissioner AB Henderson we mentioned earlier did mention a Cuba Libre made from "hot water" [read: *aguardiente de caña*] and honey. Later, the 1902 book *Farrow & Jackson Limited's Recipes for American and Other Iced Drinks* documented the existence of a drink called Rum & Honey.

Because of its unique location in the Caribbean, Cuba is blessed with abundant and varied flowers, making honey from this island more aromatic and complex in character than single-flowered varieties. It is produced throughout the island.

---

92   http://es.wikipedia.org/wiki/Canch percent C3 percent A1nchara

The healthful properties of Cuban honey combined with rum are told on the El Floridita web site, narrating that:

> The combination of two thirds of rum and one third of lemon juice was an efficient cure for the thirst of the Cuban combatants fighting against the Spanish colonial army during the second part of the 19th century. It was an excellent painkiller for the injured persons. There is why a bottle of Canchánchara was often seeing hung at the saddle of the soldiers' mount. From that time, it has been a synonym of the struggle of the Cuban people for their independence."[93]

On the same web site, El Floridita narrates a story about the birth of the Daiquirí that connects it to Canchánchara:

> In 1898 the American troops, under the command of General Shafter, landed in the south-east region of the Daiquirí area (there still a beach which bears this name near Santiago de Cuba) to intervene in the war between Cuba, Spain and the United States. The general was fat. It was impossible for him to ride a horse and had to be transported in a cart pulled by a team of horses.

In addition, Shafter made a lot of mistakes during the Cuban campaigns. In spite of

---

93   http://www.elfloridita.net/pages/Daiquirí.php?language=en

his faults, he was an inveterate gourmet. He didn't take long time to discover the preferred drink of Cuban patriots, a mixture of rum, lemon juice and sugar. Tasting it he declared: 'Only one ingredient is missing: ice'.[94]

Although commercial ice (commonly available throughout the US by the late 1800s) had been exported from Boston to Havana since 1807 by Frederic Tudor, ice was being made locally in Cuba by commercial means by the end of the century.

A syndicated item that appeared in the US press in 1898 does shed some light on conditions in Santiago de Cuba for both locals and American military forces:

> The water supply of the city, which was cut off on July 3 above El Caney by General Garcia's troops, leaving the town without water, will be turned on again tonight. The ice factory resumed work today, using the rainwater supply in the cisterns. ...All the liquor stores, wholesale and retail, are closed under General Shafter's orders, but the Spanish soldiers have a large stock of rum on hand, which they are exchanging for our hardtack and corned beef.[95]

It's no wonder that the Cuban Liberation Army was hydrating on Canchánchara. There weren't enough supplies of water or food

---

94   http://www.elfloridita.net/pages/Daiquirí.php?language=en

95   "Santiago is Filthy", *The Burlington Hawkeye*, 20 July 1898.

to properly take care of residents let alone an army. But the Cuban Liberation Army obviously had plenty of aguardiente or rum.

Consequently, the Canchánchara was more than likely present at the height of the 1898 Spanish-American War—when the town of Daiquirí became the focal point of an offensive that saw Spanish troops attacked from the land by General Calixto García's Cuban Liberation Army and from the sea by Admiral William T Sampson's American naval forces led by General William Shafter, who landed 17,000 troops on the shipping docks owned by the Spanish-American Iron Company on Daiquirí Bay.

It is possible that the same compound called Cuba Libre (reported by American journalists as "hot water and honey" translated from "burning water and honey") may have been also contained citrus juice, making it an alternate name for Canchánchara.

As a "native" compound, it is also possible that the elements inspired the creation of the Daiquirí by an American engineer who had close associations with the Cuban Liberation Army.

THE SCHIZOPHRENIC JENNINGS COX STORY

The most commonly distributed story about the Daiquirí's birth involves an 1898 meeting between Jennings Stockton Cox Jr and Francesco Domenico Pagliuchi.

New York mining engineer Jennings S Cox Jr was the general manager of the Spanish-American Iron Company, starting in 1896, and a member of the American Institute of Mining Engineers. A fellow member of the association, Francesco Domenico Pagliuchi was also an engineer. Additionally, he was a war correspondent for Harper's Monthly and was a commander in the Liberating Army of Cuba. (He wrote a detailed account of the US Navy landing at Daiquirí that was published in the 1898 Harper's Pictorial History of the War with Spain.)

When bartender Emilio "Maragato" González—famous for popularizing the Daiquirí in Havana—passed away on 30 July 1940, it was FD Pagliuchi who documented the incident of the drink's invention.

THE COX DAIQUIRÍ #1:
PAGLIUCHI'S STORY

Apparently, the editor of *El Pais* news-paper made a mistake in writing Maragato's obituary, crediting the bartender with the Daiquirí's origination. Pagliuchi sent the following correction:

Mr Director of El Pais,

Havana

My very dear sir:

In today's edition of your appreciable periodical "El Pais" I have read an article titled, "There died yesterday evening 'Maragato', the inventor of "Daiquirí." Allow me to clarify that the delicious 'Daiquirí' was not invented in Havana, but in the mines of Daiquirí, by the Engineer [Jennings S] Cox [Jr], the director of these mines.

At the conclusion of the war of independence of Cuba [in 1898], in which I had very active part, I obtained American capital to reactivate the old El Cobre copper mines situated near Santiago de Cuba, of which I was the director. While occupied in this work, I had occasion to go to Daiquirí to speak with mister Cox. Concluding the matter that I took to Daiquirí, I asked mister Cox if he was going to invite me for a cocktail.

In the sideboard of the mine's dining room, there was not gin nor vermouth; there was only Bacardí, lemons, sugar, and ice. With these elements we did a very well shaken and very cold cocktail that I liked much. Then I asked Cox: — and this: how is it called? He answered: "'Rum Sour'. In the United States there is a drink that is called a 'Whisky Sour', which is made with whisky, sugar, lemon juice and ice". But I said to him: "This name is very long, why not call it Daiquirí?"

Later, we went to Santiago de Cuba; to the bar of the American Club, where there were already a few acquaintances asking for a Daiquirí. The bar attendant answered that he did not know what it was. At that time Cox explained to him how it was made, recommending to shake it up and serve it very cold. Some of the friends who were in the bar also asked for a Daiquirí. We all liked it and very soon this cocktail made itself popular in Santiago, where from it went on to Havana and today it has a worldwide reputation. The above description is the real version of how the famous 'Daiquirí' was invented.

Your obedient servant,
Engineer FD Pagliuchi, Commander of the Liberation Army of Cuba[96]

96   Sanchez, Hilario Alonso. *El Arte del Cantinero: Los Vinos y Los Licores* (Havana: P. Hernandez y Cia, S. Inc., 1948)

It is interesting to note that in the original Spanish, Pagliuchi stated that *limones* (lemons) were used, not *limas* (limes) nor *limones criollos* (key limes).

In his 1939 food and drink travelogue, *The Gentleman's Companion*, Charles H Baker Jr added a friend of his to this cast of characters: Harry E Stout, whom he said was another mining engineer based with Cox and present at the drink's creation.

> The 2 originators were my friend Harry E Stout, now domiciled in Englewood, New Jersey, and a mining engineer associate, Mr Jennings Cox. TIME: summer of 1898. PLACE: Daiquirí... [97]

ORIGINAL CUBAN DAIQUIRÍ (BAKER VERSION)

1 whiskey glass (1 ½ oz) level full of Carta Blanca, or Carta de Oro Bacardi rum, 2 tsp of sugar, the juice of 1 ½ small green limes—strained; and very finely cracked ice.[98]

97   Baker, Charles H, Jr, *The Gentleman's Companion: Volume II, Being an Exotic Drinking Book or, Around the Word with Jigger, Beaker and Flask* (New York: Derrydale Press, 1939).

98   Baker, Charles H, Jr, *The Gentleman's Companion: Volume II, Being an Exotic Drinking Book or, Around the Word with Jigger, Beaker and Flask* (New York: Derrydale Press, 1939).

WHO WAS HARRY STOUT?

There was no Harry E Stout. But there was a Henry E Stout. According to his 1918 US passport application, Henry Eugene Stout resided outside of the United States living in Port Limon, Costa Rica (from 1901 to 1903), Yucatan, Mexico (1904 to 1905), and Felton, Cuba (1911 to October 1916). He listed his permanent as Camaguey, Cuba, where he was the general shop foreman for the Cuba Railroad, an American Corporation.[99]

At the time of his 1918 application, he had retired from his job as a mechanic and planned to visit relatives living in Audobon NJ.[100]

Thus he was not an engineer as described by Baker. It is possible that before he moved to Costa Rico he had travelled to Cuba. But there is no record of him on any passenger lists sailing from the US.

---

99   Department Passport Application 28483. National Archives and Records Administration (NARA); Washington D.C.; Passport Applications, January 2, 1906 - March 31, 1925; Collection Number: ARC Identifier 583830 / MLR Number A1 534; NARA Series: M1490; Roll #: 560.

100   Department Passport Application 28483. National Archives and Records Administration (NARA); Washington D.C.; Passport Applications, January 2, 1906 - March 31, 1925; Collection Number: ARC Identifier 583830 / MLR Number A1 534; NARA Series: M1490; Roll #: 560.

NECESSITY IS THE MOTHER
OF A VARIATION ON A WHISKEY SOUR

Based on Pagliuchi's account, the recipe for a Daiquirí, or Rum Sour, would have read like a Whiskey Sour recipe from the same period:

WHISKEY SOUR

1/2 tablespoonful of sugar;
3 or 4 dashes of lemon juice;
1 squirt of syphon selter water, dissolve the sugar and lemon well with a spoon
Fill the glass with ice;
1 wine glass of whiskey:
Stir up well, strain into a sour glass;
Place your fruit into it, and serve.[101]

It could also have been made in a similar fashion to a Medford Rum Sour:

MEDFORD RUM SOUR

(Use a large bar glass.)
1/2 tablespoonful of sugar;
3 or 4 dashes of lemon juice;
1 squirt of syphon selter, dissolved well
1 wine glass of Medford rum;
Fill I of the glass with ice.

---

101   Johnson, Harry, *The Bartenders' Manual, Revised Edition* (New York: Harry Johnson, 1900).

Stir well with a spoon strain into a sour glass,
ornament with fruit, etc., and serve.
This is an old Boston drink, and has the reputation of
being cooling and pleasant.[102]

> Another version that did not include
> a squirt of soda water called a Columbia Skin
> came even closer to the Daiquirí formula:

COLUMBIA SKIN

1 teaspoonful sugar, dissolve with a little water;
1 slice of lemon;
2 or 3 pieces of broken ice;
1 wine glass of Medford rum;
Stir up well with a spoon; grate a little nutmeg on top
and serve.
This drink is called Columbia Skin by the Boston
people.[103]

> In all of these recipes, the Sour was
> stirred. Does this means that the "original"
> Daiquirí was not a shaken drink, but a stirred
> compound? Not necessarily. Both methods were
> employed in making Sours during the period.
>   The combination of rum, lemon juice,
> and sugar had already achieve almost mythical
> status, by 1884, as evidenced by an item that

---

102   Johnson, Harry, *The Bartenders' Manual, Revised Edition* (New York: Harry Johnson, 1900).

103   Johnson, Harry, *The Bartenders' Manual, Revised Edition* (New York: Harry Johnson, 1900).

associated the St. Bernard dog with this life-saving compound:

> Everyone is familiar with the myth of St Bernard dogs. ...It is popularly believed that on every stormy night he monks of St Bernard send out a dog to look for belated travellers. The dog carries a blanket, two bottles of hot water, a mustard plaster, two coarse towels, a lunch basket filled with roast chicken and three kinds of vegetables, kept hot by a spirit lamp, and a liquor case containing rum, lemon peel, sugar, and water.[104]

There is a minor problem with Pagliuchi's account. There was an Anglo-American Club in Santiago de Cuba, not an American Club. The American Club was situated in Havana and was formed in 1901.[105]

So the Daiquirí—in an American's eyes—was simply a Rum Sour made with Cuban rum instead of the more familiar Medford or Caldwell's Old Newburyport Rum which had a huge share of the American market.

Francesco Domenico Pagliuchi's correction of the *El Pais* obituary about Emilio "Maragato" González provides strong evidence that there was more than one Daiquirí being

---

104   "The St Bernard Myth", *The New York Times*, 24 October 1884.

105   Perez, Louis A, Jr, *On Becoming Cuban: Identity, Nationality, and Culture* (Chapel Hill: University of North Carolina Press, 2008) p 396.

praised around the world. His beloved Cox Daiquirí was made with lemons and mixed according to a classic Sour recipe. The other Daiquirí, the Bacardí Daiquirí used limes and offered the grenadine option.

Pagliuchi's defence of the Cox Daiquirí means that the story surrounding the Daiquirí served by Maragato might have followed the Bacardí Daiquirí recipe. But he felt strongly enough about the subject to write the editor even though he had emigrated to the US by 1905 via London and travelled frequently to Venezuela until he relocated from New York to Los Angeles.[106]

THE COX DAIQUIRÍ #2: BACARDÍ'S VERSION

Another version of the Jennings S Cox Jr story was circulated, during the 1930s, by Facundo M Bacardí, who was one of Don Facundo Bacardí y Massó's younger sons:

Shortly after the Spanish-American was, there was a popular trysting place in Santiago, known as the Venus bar. One day a group of American engineers who had come into town from the Daiquirí mines were imbibing their favourite drinks in this restful

106   Form for Naturalized Citizen, No. 77735, 17 December 1917.

spot. ...A jovial fellow by the name of Cox spoke up. "Caballeros y amigos, we have been enjoying this delicious mixture for some time, but strange to admit the drink has no name. Don't you think it is about time something was done to extricate us from this sad predicament?" It was unanimously agreed that the drink should be named without further procrastination. There was silence for several minutes as each man became immersed in deep thought. Suddenly Cox's voice was heard again. "I have it, men! Let's call it the 'Daiquirí'." and so it was named.[107]

The recipe that the Venus Bar allegedly made in those days, as related by Facundo was as follows:

The juice of half a large, or one small lime was squeezed into a shaker containing one teaspoonful of granulated sugar. Two ounces of Ron Bacardi (Carte Blanca) were added and a generous quantity of shaved ice prepared the shaker for frosting. When the mixture was thoroughly frapped it was then poured (not strained) into a chilled glass known as a "flute".[108]

107   "Origin Is Disclosed of Daiquiri Cocktail: One of Group of American Engineers Named the Drink at Santiago Bar", *The Miami Herald*, 14 March 1937.

108   "Origin Is Disclosed of Daiquiri Cocktail: One of Group of American Engineers Named the Drink at Santiago Bar", *The Miami Herald*, 14 March 1937.

Facundo also attributed the recipe blessed by him and christened the Bacardí Cocktail to the work of Eddie Woelke, when he was still mixing at the Sevilla-Biltmore Hotel. [109]

It is interesting to note that the introductory sentence to this Daiquirí story states that "The most renowned of all Cuban drinks is the Daiquirí or Bacardí cocktail." And the last paragraph echoes the point again: "The Daiquirí and Bacardí Cocktails are the same." (We will discuss this point in more detail later.)

Another two facts are added to the drink's development in this article. Facundo Bacardí states that Eddie Woelke improved this version of the drink by using cracked ice instead of shaved ice and straining it into a cocktail glass. According to Bacardí, it was Woelke who named his version the Bacardí Cocktail. This means that the drink was named such sometime after 1919 when Woelke first went behind the bar at the Sevilla-Biltmore Hotel.

This makes the story as Facundo related more myth than fact. The Bacardí Cocktail with grenadine appeared in Jacques Straub 1914 book *Drinks*.

109   "Origin Is Disclosed of Daiquiri Cocktail: One of Group of American Engineers Named the Drink at Santiago Bar", *The Miami Herald*, 14 March 1937.

BACARDI COCKTAIL (STRAUB VERSION)

½ pony grenadine syrup.
2/3 jigger Bacardi rum.
Juice of half a lime.
Shake well. Strain. Serve.[110]

THE EYEWITNESSES

According to the entry for the town of Daiquirí in Wikipedia, the list of those present at the naming of this drink included: J Francis Linthicum, C Manning Combs, George W Pfeiffer, De Berneire Whitaker, C Merritt Holmes and Proctor O Persing. [111]

No mention is made of either Francesco Domenico Pagliuchi nor of Charles H Baker Jr's friend Henry Eugene Stout.

All of the men listed could have been present in the years immediately following the Spanish-American War. But it is difficult to say if they were definitely in the area, especially De Bernier Whitaker and C Merritt Holmes, whose names do not appear on any passenger lists for people sailing to or from Cuba during that period.

---

110   Straub, Jacques. *Drinks* (Chicago: Marie L Straub; The hotel Monthly Press, 1914).

111   http://en.wikipedia.org/wiki/Daiquirí

However, incoming passenger records do show that Chemist J Francis Linthicum, age 27, sailed on 21 October 1911 from Antilla, Cuba on board the *SS Thames* headed for New York.[112]

Miner C Manning Combs, age 35, sailed on 21 July 1908 from Santiago de Cuba on the *SS Vigilancia* headed for New York.[113]

George W Pfeiffer, age 37, whose occupation was not included on the passenger, sailed on 6 October 1907, from Havana on the *SS Saratoga* headed for New York; on 26 September 1913, on board the *SS Carl Schurz* from Santiago de Cuba, where his US address was listed as the Engineers Club, Philadelphia, Pennsylvania, headed for New York; and lastly on 4 July 1916 on board the *SS Titives* headed for New York.[114]

The person of most interest, however, is Proctor O Persing, age 33, who sailed on 15 September 1911 from Santiago de Cuba on the *SS Prinz August Wilhelm* bound for New York.

112   "Passenger Lists of Vessels Arriving at New York, New York, 1820-1897" (National Archives Microfilm Publication M237, 675 rolls); Records of the U.S. Customs Service, Record Group 36; National Archives, Washington, D.C.

113   "Passenger Lists of Vessels Arriving at New York, New York, 1820-1897" (National Archives Microfilm Publication M237, 675 rolls); Records of the U.S. Customs Service, Record Group 36; National Archives, Washington, D.C.

114   "Passenger Lists of Vessels Arriving at New York, New York, 1820-1897" (National Archives Microfilm Publication M237, 675 rolls); Records of the U.S. Customs Service, Record Group 36; National Archives, Washington, D.C.

Even though he made two subsequent trips, this one voyage carried two other passengers— a "student" named Facundo Bacardí, age 21, and Arturo Schueg, age 15, who was son of Henri Schueg, Emilio Bacardí's brother-in-law and the man who was largely responsible for the company's international marketing strategy.[115]

The young Bacardí possibly heard the tale from older Proctor Persing whilst sailing to the New York. More than likely the Venus Hotel Bar crafted a version that resonated with its patrons. But from Bacardí's accounts of the recipes, these drinks may have contained the same ingredients, but by execution were not from the Sour family of compounds described by Pagliuchi.

THE COX DAIQUIRÍ #3: BACARDÍ STORY #2

A more recent version of the story that has circulated in print and on the internet includes a hand-written version of the recipe that was purportedly produced by Jennings S Cox Jr and handed out to patrons.

115　"Passenger Lists of Vessels Arriving at New York, New York, 1820-1897" (National Archives Microfilm Publication M237, 675 rolls); Records of the U.S. Customs Service, Record Group 36; National Archives, Washington, D.C.

DAIQUIRÍ ("MR COX" VERSION)

(for 6 persons)

The juice of 6 lemons

6 teaspoons of sugar

6 Bacardí cups— "Carta Blanca"

2 small cups of mineral water

Plenty of crushed ice

Put all ingredients in a cocktail shaker and shake well. Do not strain as the glass may be served with some ice. [116]

The writing in the upper right corner is curious. If this was handwritten and distributed by Cox, why does it say "original" and "Mr

116   "Daiquiri", http://www.havanaturbahamas.com/drinks.html

Cox's"?[117] This is not a usual statement of first-person authorship. According to the Diffords-Guide database, this recipe allegedly came from Jennings Cox Jr's personal diary.[118] But if this piece paper came from his personal diary, why does "Original Mr Cox" appear in the corner of what is obviously an index card.

But then Difford also states in the same entry that "US Admiral Lucius Johnson fought in the Spanish-American War." This fact will be played out later in this report as being false.

Another problem with Difford's entry is that he mentions that "Cox's granddaughter recounts a slightly different tale; namely that Cox ran out of gin when entertaining American guests. Wary of serving them straight rum, he added lime and sugar. However Cox came to concoct the drink, the result was sublime."

When Jennings and Isabel Cox sailed to New York on 2 May 1913 on board the *SS Prinz Joachim*, the 46- and 44-year-old couple

---

117   The image above of the "original Cox's recipe" has appeared throughout the internet blogs ever since National Daiquirí Day (July 19) was announced in 2006 by Bacardí's public relations agency of record, Corbin & Associates Limited,who took over the brand from the Baddish Group, the agency responsible for promoting the Mojito during the 1990s. Although this is not a government-sanctioned nor presidential-decreed national day such as National ice Cream, which also takes place on the third Sunday of July, the PR agency has continued promoting the "original" Daiquirí using this image.

118   http://www.diffordsguide.com/site/main/welcome.jsp?cocktailId=611

was not accompanied by any children.[119] Even in his 1913 obituary, Cox was survived by only his father and his wife.[120] We will go further into Jennings S Cox Jr's final years in a moment.

This fact can also be discounted because Cox apparently had no children.

The story attached to this "discovered" piece of evidence obviously has a few flaws.

However, this Daiquirí recipe does agree with Pagliuchi's account that uses lemons [*limons*], not limes [*limas*] or key limes [*limones criollos*]. And it blatantly conflicts with the recipes narrated by Facundo Bacardí during the 1930s and with any recipes issued by Bacardí in their marketing and promotional materials ever since.

THE COX DAIQUIRÍ #4: THE G SELMER FOUGNER STORY

In 1935, a journalist the *New York Sun* newspaper, G Selmer Fougner, compiled and published material for his "Along the Wine Trail" columns into a book.

---

119   "Passenger Lists of Vessels Arriving at New York, New York, 1820-1897" (National Archives Microfilm Publication M237, 675 rolls); Records of the U.S. Customs Service, Record Group 36; National Archives, Washington, D.C.

120   "Obituaries: Jennings S Cox Jr" *The New York Times*, 2 September 1913.

Hoping to educate a new generation of post-Prohibition drinkers who knew nothing of the history of distillation and popular drinks, Fougner detailed numerous "lost" cocktails. What was his take of the birth of the Daiquirí?

Jennings S Cox, inventor of the famous Daiquirí, was strongly opposed to called the drink a "cocktail." From long years spent in Cuba, he held strongly to the theory that the wise traveller should, so far as possible, confine himself to the food and drink native to the country in which he chanced to be. And the Daiquirí, for that reason was, in his opinion, the ideal Cuban drink.

Mr Cox was meticulousness itself in the care with which he prepared the Daiquirí—"one of lime, two of sugar, and three of Bacardí." All the ingredients having been thoroughly mixed, the lime juice and sugar separately, the fluid result was poured over finely cracked ice packed in a champagne glass.[121]

DAIQUIRÍ (FOUGNER VERSION)

½ oz lime juice
2 teaspoons sugar
1 ½ oz Bacardí
Stir ingredients over ice and strain into a champagne glass packed with finely cracked ice.

---

121   Fougner, G Selmar. *Along the Wine Trail: An Anthology of Wines and Spirits* (Boston: The Stratford Company, 1935)

Did Fougner interview Cox? Where did the echo of the classic punch recipe come into play? "One of lime, two of sugar, and three of Bacardí"?

If we are to believe the statement that Cox felt that one should "confine himself to the food and drink native to the country in which he chanced to be" then the compass points true in the relationship between the Canchánchara and the Daiquirí.

THE FATE OF JENNINGS STOCKTON COX JR

Jennings S Cox Jr travelled quite frequently from Cuba to New York where his stockbroker father Jennings S Cox lived at 170 West 73 Street and later at 140 West 71 Street in Manhattan.[122]

The younger Cox appears in passenger lists from 1904, 1906, 1907, 1909, and 1910. His wife Ysabel, a native Cuban who was born in Santiago de Cuba, frequently joined him.[123]

---

122   Thirteenth Census of the United States, 1910 (NARA microfilm publication T624, 1,178 rolls). Records of the Bureau of the Census, Record Group 29. National Archives, Washington, D.C.

123   Passenger and Crew Lists of Vessels Arriving at New York, New York, 1897-1957; (National Archives Microfilm Publication T715, 8892 rolls); Records of the Immigration and Naturalization Service; National Archives, Washington, D.C.

His final trip to the land of his birth occurred in 1913. According to the passenger record of the *SS Prinz Joachim*, the 46-year-old Jennings S Cox Jr returned to New York for the last time on 2 May 1913 from Santiago de Cuba.

He died at his father's home on 31 August 1913, which was reported in the 2 September and 13 September editions of *The New York Times*, survived only by his wife and his father.[124]

FINALLY, THE KEY LIME APPEARS: THE CANTINEROS' DAIQUIRÍ

In the 1948 edition of *El Arte del Cantinero*, the "approved" cantinero association recipe for the Daiquirí did not specifically call for Bacardí rum:

DAIQUIRÍ (1948 VERSION)

1 shot Cuban rum
2 teaspoons sugar
Juice of a medium-sized key lime [read: limon criollo].
Ice. Shake 25 times, strain, and serve. If the customer desires add 3 dashes of grenadine syrup.[125]

---

124 "Jennings S. Cox, Jr." *The New York Times*, 2 September 1913; "Obituaries"" *The New York Times*, 13 September 1913.

125 Sanchez, Hilario Alonso. *El Arte del Cantinero: Los Vinos y Los Licores* (Havana: P. Hernandez y Cia, S. Inc., 1948)

This is not the recipe for a Daiquirí as shown in earlier accounts from either Pagliuchi or Bacardí. It includes the option of adding grenadine. Neither does it call for Bacardí rum, just Cuban rum.

However, the two Bacardí cocktails do make the distinct brand call. But the drinks do not call for *limon criollo*. They call for *limon*:

BACARDI NO. 1 (1948 VERSION)

1 teaspoon sugar
1 shot Bacardí Rum
Juice of half a lemon
Ice. Shake well, strain, and serve. [126]

BACARDI NO. 2 (1948 VERSION)

4 parts Bacardí Rum
1 part grenadine syrup
1 part lemon juice
Ice. Shake 35 times, strain, and serve.[127]

An earlier Cuban cocktail book, *El Arte de Hacer un Cocktail y Algo Más*, published in 1927, did not specify the brand of rum to be used in either the Daiquirí or the Daiquirí Dulce.

---

126   Sanchez, Hilario Alonso. *El Arte del Cantinero: Los Vinos y Los Licores* (Havana: P. Hernandez y Cia, S. Inc., 1948)

127   Sanchez, Hilario Alonso. *El Arte del Cantinero: Los Vinos y Los Licores* (Havana: P. Hernandez y Cia, S. Inc., 1948)

DAIQUIRI (1927 VERSION)

3 parts rum
Juice of half a lemon
1 teaspoon sugar
Shake and serve.[128]

DAIQUIRI DULCE (1927 VERSION)

½ rum
½ lemon juice
a little grenadine syrup
Shake and serve.[129]

From these Cuban recipes we can clearly see that a Sweet Daiquirí may have been embraced by the Bacardí company because it resonated with consumers who were largely American tourists and journalists.

Hence, in the minds of Cuban bartenders during the 1940s, there were two Barcadí Cocktails: one was a Daiquirí made with Bacardí, the other was a Sweet Daiquirí that included grenadine.

---

128   *El Arte de Hacer un Cocktail y Algo Mas* (Havana: Compañia Cervecera International SA, 1927; Cheltenham: Mixellany Limited, 2011)

129   *El Arte de Hacer un Cocktail y Algo Mas* (Havana: Compañia Cervecera International SA, 1927; Cheltenham: Mixellany Limited, 2011)

LAST BUT NOT LEAST: THE ESCALANTE DAIQUIRÍ

John B Escalante, proprietor of the Grand Hotel in Matanzas, confuses the situation even further. His 1915 recipe calls for grenadine and curaçao.

DAIQUIRI COCKTAIL (1915 VERSION)

1 green lemon [read: lime], juiced
1 teaspoon granulated sugar
1 teaspoon grenadine
1 teaspoon curaçao
45 ml Ron Bacardí
Shake and serve as a frappe in a Champagne coupe.[130]

Even before Constante Ribalaigua Vert developed his world famous Daiquirí Frappé (also known as Daiquirí No. 4 [Howard and Mae]) and its four siblings, there was no consensus in the cocktail world as to how to make a Daiquirí.

However, the execution of Escalante's version does match the method prescribed by the Venus Hotel bar as told by Facundo M Bacardí.

---

130   Escalante, John B. *Manuel del Cantinero* (Havana: Imprénta Moderna, 1915).

THE DAIQUIRÍ
SWEEPS AMERICAN SHORES

According to numerous online sources, the plaque at the Daiquirí Lounge in the Army & Navy Club in Washington DC proudly cites that in 1909 Admiral Lucius W Johnson met Jennings S Cox Jr in Cuba. He was so taken by the recipe that he brought home an ample supply of rum and introduced it to the exclusive military officers club.

There are flaws in this statement.

According to his 1968 obituary, Rear Admiral Lucius W Johnson was only a Lieutenant in the US Navy Medical Corps when he entered the service, in 1908, fresh from his "internship at Blockley [Hospital]". [131]

And the only plaque that is displayed on the Army & Navy Club website curiously states that the Daiquirí Lounge was founded in 1885. The club itself was founded in December 1885 as the United Service Club and was reincorporated on 15 October 1891 as the Army & Navy Club.[132] We cannot locate photos of the plaque that commemorates Johnson's introduction of the drink in the club. But the club, at one time, gave its Daiquirí recipe on its website:

---

131   "Obituary: Read Admiral Lucius W. Johnson, MC, USN (Ret.) 1882-1968", *Plastic & Reconstructive Surgery*, Volume 41, Issue 6, June 1968.

132   A photo of the plaque the commemorates Johnson's introduction of the drink in the club was not available at the time of this writing.

ARMY & NAVY CLUB DAIQUIRÍ

A Glass, a jigger of rum, the juice of half a lime, a
teaspoon of sugar, finely shaved ice and a good stir.
No bitters!—and no better in town! Visit the lounge
for a pre- or- post dinner drink, or for an after work
wind down.[133]

As of this writing, this recipe no longer
appears on the club's website. But if this is the
recipe that Lucius Johnson learnt from Jennings
S Cox Jr and not from some other source, then
the use of sparkling mineral water and the Rum
Sour concept have to be altogether discounted!

THE FIRST PUBLISHED RECIPE
IN THE US FOR THE DAIQUIRÍ

So when did the Daiquirí recipe first
make an appearance in print? Former "wine
steward" at the Blackstone Hotel in Chicago and
the Pendennis Club in Louisville KY, Jacques
Straub documented in 1914 a few hundred
mixed drinks that were popular before the First
World War. Among them was a Daiguiri [sic]
that featured the lime juice more than the rum.
(The Bacardí Cocktail that featured the grenadine syrup was presented early in this chapter.)

---

133   http://www.armynavyclub.org/Default.aspx?p=DynamicModule&pagei
d=236584&ssid=90237&vnf=1, recipe captured in November 2010.

DAIGUIRI (STRAUB VERSION)

1/3 jigger lime juice
2/3 jigger rum
1 bar spoon powdered sugar
Shake well with fine ice; strain into cocktail glass.[134]

The recipes are found again two years later in another book.

Head bartender for the Hotel Wallick in New York City, Hugo R Ensslin documented, in 1916, an interesting trio of exceptions to the Daiquirí, the Cuban Cocktail, and the Bacardí Cocktail recipes:

CUBAN COCKTAIL (ENSSLIN VERSION)

1 jigger Bacardí Rum
2 dashes Gum Syrup
Juice of 1/2 Lime
Shake well in a mixing glass with cracked ice, strain and serve.[135]

BACARDÍ COCKTAIL (ENSSLIN VERSION)

1 drink Bacardí Rum
Juice of 1/2 Lime
2 dashes Gum Syrup

---

134   Straub, Jacques. *Drinks* (Chicago: Marie L Straub; The hotel Monthly Press, 1914).

135   Ensslin, Hugo R. *Recipes for Mixed Drinks* (New York: Fox printing House, 1916).

Shake well in a mixing glass with cracked ice, strain
and serve. [136]

DAIGUIRI COCKTAIL
(ENSSLIN VERSION)

1 jigger Bacardí Rum
2 dashes Grenadine Syrup
Juice of 1 Lime
Shake well in a mixing glass with cracked ice, strain
and serve in a cocktail glass. [137]

At first glance, it appears that Ensslin
got the Daiquirí and Bacardí recipes confused.
The Cuban Cocktail appears to be only a reitera-
tion of his Bacardí Cocktail—or did he mean
Daiquirí?

How did Ensslin learn of the Daiquirí,
the Bacardí, and the Cuban?

It looks as if the Bacardí sales team visited the Hotel Wallick, introducing the use of
lime juice and Bacardí that no longer made it
the Rum Sour that Jennings S Cox Jr and FD
Pagliuchi savoured.

---

136   Ensslin, Hugo R. *Recipes for Mixed Drinks* (New York: Fox printing
House, 1916).

137   Ensslin, Hugo R. *Recipes for Mixed Drinks* (New York: Fox printing
House, 1916).

WHICH ONE IS IT?
A DAIQUIRÍ OR A BACARDÍ COCKTAIL?

Let's go back to the Bacardí Cocktail—
a Daiquirí with the addition of grenadine—for
a moment. Remember the 1937 *Miami Herald*
article about the origins of the Daiquirí that was
previously mentioned? There are two fascinating
statements at the end of that reporter's piece:

> During prohibition this drink was pitifully abused.
> Many establishments used grenadine in place of
> sugar, and this still obtains today. There is a cocktail
> called Santiago which requires no sweetening, but is
> absolutely wrong to give it the name Daiquirí.
>
> ...
> The Daiquirí and Bacardí cocktails are the same.[138]

The Bacardí Cocktail was so popular
after Prohibition's repeal it was served along with
Daiquirí everywhere and not always made with
Bacardí, even at the hotel where the company's
sales marketing director Fausto Rodriguez resided in 1936, the Barbizon-Plaza Hotel in New
York's Upper East Side.

According to a 1996 *Cigar Aficionado*
article, the landmark decision, which dictated

---

138   "Origin Is Disclosed of Daiquiri Cocktail: One of Group of American
Engineers Named the Drink at Santiago Bar", *The Miami Herald*, 14 March
1937.

that a Bacardí Cocktail must be made with Bacardí rum was used in an advertising campaign:

> The museum in Miami also exhibits the company's old ads, including one that commemorates a 1936 decision by the appellate division of the New York Supreme Court that a Bacardí cocktail (Bacardí Light, lime juice, sugar and grenadine) wasn't a Bacardí cocktail unless it was made with Bacardí rum. Bacardí lawyers had called dozens of bartenders to testify in the case, bringing them in from all over the world. They supported the company's argument, [Peter] Foster writes, 'by stating that no self-respecting barman would serve anything else in a Bacardí cocktail.' [139]

New York Supreme Court Justice Rosenman ruled against the company's claim against the Barbizon-Plaza Hotel (where national sales manager Fausto Rodriguez resided) and the Wivel Restaurant, stating that "The plaintiff does not how sufficient clearness to warrant a temporary injunction that in practice and understanding Bacardi cocktails must necessarily contain the product of the plaintiff."[140]

Besides, a number of other drinks received Supreme Court rulings long before the Bacardí cocktail. For example, Heublein sued the

---

[139]   Benes, Alejandro, "Spirit of the Bat: The Rum Dynasty: Bacardí" *Cigar Aficionado*, 1 September 1996.

[140]   "LOSES COCKTAIL SUIT: Bacardi Firm Fails to Prove Use of Its Rum Is Essential." *The New York Times*, 31 January 1936.

Adams Company in Massachusetts in 1903, and successfully in US Supreme Court in 1904 for infringing on its Club Cocktails trademarked name.[141]

Despite the Bacardí Cocktail's popularity in the US, the Bacardí Daiquirí was the headliner in Havana when the company opened its free bar in the Bacardí Building in 1931, American journalists were treated to a Daiquirí (touted as the national drink).[142] Not a Bacardí Cocktail.

Was it that consumers didn't favour the use of grenadine any longer? Possibly.

Nevertheless, Bacardí attempted to trademark the name "Daiquirí Bacardí" in the US for a "liquor with a rum base known generically as 'Daiquirí.'" The application was turned down by the US Commissioner of Patents based on opposition filed by Compania Ron Daiquirí SV of Havana on 22 January 1935.[143] At the time, Ron Daiquirí was making headway, exporting its product to the US and Britain, where it was being adopted by key influencers such as the Savoy's Harry Craddock and UKBG President William J Tarling.[144]

141　Heublein v Adams, CCMass 1903; 125 Fed. 785, 1904.

142　"Another Free Bar in Havana", *San Antonio Light*, 10 October 1931.

143　"Decision of the Commissioner of Patents: Descriptive Terms", *The Trade-mark Reporter*, Vol 25, Issue 2, 1935.

144　It is interesting to note that Tarling's 1937 book presented 49 recipes that contained Daiquiri Rum. Tarling, William J. *Café Royal Cocktail Book* (London: Pall Mall, Ltd, 1937; Cheltenham: Mixellany Limited, 2009).

KING'S JUBILEE

Invented by Harry Craddock

¼ Lemon Juice.

¼ Luxardo's Maraschino (Dry).

½ Daiquiri Rum.

Shake and strain into cocktail glass.[145]

CUBAN MANHATTAN

½ Daiquiri Rum.

½ Martini Sweet Vermouth.

2 dashes Angostura Bitters.[146]

DAIQUIRÍ (1937 VERSION)

3 dashes Gomme Syrup.

¾ Daiquiri Rum.

¼ Juice of a Lime or Lemon.

Shake.[147]

DAIQUIRÍ BLOSSOM

½ Orange Juice.

½ Daiquiri Rum.

1 dash Maraschino.

Shake and strain. [148]

---

145   Tarling, William J. *Café Royal Cocktail Book* (London: Pall Mall, Ltd, 1937; Cheltenham: Mixellany Limited, 2009).

146   Tarling, William J. *Café Royal Cocktail Book* (London: Pall Mall, Ltd, 1937; Cheltenham: Mixellany Limited, 2009).

147   Tarling, William J. *Café Royal Cocktail Book* (London: Pall Mall, Ltd, 1937; Cheltenham: Mixellany Limited, 2009).

148   Tarling, William J. *Café Royal Cocktail Book* (London: Pall Mall, Ltd, 1937; Cheltenham: Mixellany Limited, 2009).

DAIQUIRÍ GRAPEFRUIT BLOSSOM

1/3 Grapefruit Juice.
2/3 Daiquiri Rum.
3 dashes Maraschino.
Shake and strain. [149]

DAIQUIRÍ LIBERAL

2/3 Daiquiri Rum.
1/3 Martini Sweet Vermouth.
1 dash Amer Picon.
Use mixing glass. [150]

DAIQUIRÍ OLD-FASHIONED

1 dash Angostura Bitters.
2 dashes Orange Bitters.
1 lump of Sugar dissolved in two spoonsful of Water.
1 glass Daiquiri Rum.
Serve in an old-fashioned glass and serve with fruit
and mint. [151]

DAIQUIRÍ SPECIAL

1 teaspoonful Grenadine.
1/3 Gin.
2/3 Daiquiri Rum
The Juice of ½ Lime

149   Tarling, William J. *Café Royal Cocktail Book* (London: Pall Mall, Ltd, 1937; Cheltenham: Mixellany Limited, 2009).

150   Tarling, William J. *Café Royal Cocktail Book* (London: Pall Mall, Ltd, 1937; Cheltenham: Mixellany Limited, 2009).

151   Tarling, William J. *Café Royal Cocktail Book* (London: Pall Mall, Ltd, 1937; Cheltenham: Mixellany Limited, 2009).

Shake and strain into cocktail glass. [152]

FAIR & WARMER

1/3 Italian Vermouth.
2/3 Daiquiri Rum.
2 dashes Curasao [sic].
Mix and strain into cocktail glass. [153]

Marketed as a cocktail rum, Daiquirí Rum from Compania Ron Daiquirí SV did venture after the American market during the 1930s. And like other Cuban rum distilleries in the early post-Prohibition years, the company also fought for market share by establishing a Puerto Rican distillery to take advantage of the tariff-free export of rums from American territories.

The alleged landmark lawsuit had more to do with the fact that if Compania Ron Daiquirí could stop them from using the word "Daiquirí" coupled with Bacardí, then they could stop anyone from making a Bacardí Cocktail without Bacardí!

However, the conflict may not have started in the US. It may have first erupted in Havana.

152   Tarling, William J. *Café Royal Cocktail Book* (London: Pall Mall, Ltd, 1937; Cheltenham: Mixellany Limited, 2009).

153   Tarling, William J. *Café Royal Cocktail Book* (London: Pall Mall, Ltd, 1937; Cheltenham: Mixellany Limited, 2009).

THE HAVANA CLUB SPECIAL

With the promotional push in Havana of the Daiquirí by Bacardí, the José Arechabala SA's Havana Club brand chose a different name for its version of the Daiquirí when in 1934 it opened its "private club bar". The company publicised its Havana Club Special "Frozen Cocktail" on its complimentary admission cards.

HAVANA CLUB SPECIAL

1 tsp sugar
½ oz lime or lemon juice
1 oz Havana Club Rum
Dissolve lime juice and sugar first in the cocktail shaker. Add Havana Club Rum and cracked ice according to number of cocktails to be mixed. Shake this mixture until it is frozen.

"COMPLIMENTS OF HAVANA CLUB RUM"
"HAVANA CLUB SPECIAL"
FROZEN COCKTAIL
TO BE MADE WITH
HAVANA CLUB RUM
1 TEASPOON FULL OF SUGAR
½ OZ. LIME OR LEMON JUICE
1 OZ. HAVANA CLUB RUM
DISSOLVE LIME JUICE AND SUGAR FIRST, IN THE COCKTAIL SHAKER.
ADD HAVANA CLUB RUM AND CRACKED ICE ACCORDING TO NUM-
BER OF COCKTAILS TO BE MIXED. SHAKE THIS MIXTURE UNTIL IT
IS FROZEN.

HAVANA CLUB RUM Bldg.

◆ Opposite to Columbus
Cathedral Havana Cuba

You are cordially invited as our guest to visit our private Club and Bar and to try our "Havana Club Special" frozen "Cocktail" made with our famous Havana Club Rum.

Our building formerly the home of the Count of Bayona, remains exactly as it was 200 years ago.

You will admire the handsome Old Cuban "Patio" the mahogany ceilings, marble floors, antique crystal chandeliers, etc.

Lemon or lime juice was suggested in the recipe. This was smart marketing on the part of Havana Club, especially since Compania Ron Daiquirí had its sights set on suing Bacardí for infringement of the name Daiquirí.

Why was there an option for lemon or lime juice?

Americans living in the Midwest and the North were not accustomed to the taste of limes. Until the late twentieth century, limes were hard to come by in those regions, had a limited growing season even in Florida, and were not a familiar taste.

Lemonade was more popular than limeade. And for those who enjoyed the Cox Daiquirí made with lemons, Havana Club offered American tourists a near equivalent.

WHERE DID THE GRENADINE GO?

After the case for the Bacardí Cocktail was won in court, in 1936, it seem that the company's American marketing team decided that grenadine should no longer be in the compound This is evident by the comments found not only in the 1937 *Miami Herald* article, but from the narrative given by Jack Townsend in his 1951 *The Bartender's Book*:

> If you can detect any difference between a Daiquirí and a Bacardí mixed according to the original recipe—aside from the brand of rum used—we will be glad to pin a miniature bar cuspidor on your lapel. ... But the Bacardí is the only mixed drink whose ingredients are specified by a decision of the Supreme Court of New York State....According to the expert testimony of the late Eddie Woelke, when grenadine is added, the Bacardí becomes a Santiago.[154]

SANTIAGO COCKTAIL (TOWNSEND VERSION)

2 Dashes Grenadine
2 Dashes Lemon Juice
1 Glass Bacardi Rum

---

154   Townsend, Jack and McBride, Tom Moore, *The Bartender's Book* (New York: Penguin Group, 1951).

Shake well and strain into cocktail glass. [155]

Townsend went on to record the following recipes for a Daiquirí and a Bacardí:

DAIQUIRI COCKTAIL
(TOWNSEND VERSION)

1 ½ oz rum
Juice of half lime
1 teaspoon sugar
Shake well with ice. Strain into cocktail glass. [156]

BACARDI COCKTAIL
(TOWNSEND VERSION)

1 ½ oz rum
Juice of half lime
1 teaspoon sugar
Shake well with ice. Strain into cocktail glass. [157]

Even Bacardí's US distributor, Schenley Products Company of New York, deleted the grenadine syrup in the Bacardí Cocktail that used in its 1938 marketing campaign.[158]

---

155   Townsend, Jack and McBride, Tom Moore, *The Bartender's Book* (New York: Penguin Group, 1951).

156   Townsend, Jack and McBride, Tom Moore, *The Bartender's Book* (New York: Penguin Group, 1951).

157   Townsend, Jack and McBride, Tom Moore, *The Bartender's Book* (New York: Penguin Group, 1951).

158   "Schenley's Merry Mixer", Schenley Products Company of New York, 1938.

BACARDI COCKTAIL (SCHENLEY VERSION)

Juice of ½ green lime
1/2 teaspoon granulated sugar
1 jigger Bacardí White Label
Shake well with finely shipped ice and pour into
cocktail glass. [159]

Wait a minute!

The Daiquirí and the Bacardí Cocktail were one in the same in many people's minds? And Eddie Woelke, who Facundo Bacardí claimed was the inventor of the Bacardí Cocktail simply because he strained a Daiquirí made with Bacardí, called the grenadine version a Santiago?

Why didn't Bacardí correct these convolutions and misstatements since they had won the right to claim the Bacardí Cocktail as proprietary compound?

It seems that the company took a different tact by the 1950s. The marketing team headed up by Fausto Rodriguez pushed a recipe for a Dry Daiquirí in the US as a PUERTO RICAN rum drink in its newspaper ad campaign.[160]

---

159   "Schenley's Merry Mixer", Schenley Products Company of New York, 1938.

160   "Taste the Difference Dry Rum Makes!", *The Milwaukee Journal*, 10 August 1956.

DRY DAIQUIRI

1 ½ ounces Puerto Rican rum
½ ounce fresh lime juice
Sugar to taste
Then shake like the dickens with cracked ice.[161]

Replacing Cuban rum with Puerto Rican rum did not suit David Embury's very exacting opinion about the Daiquirí, as he commented:

...I pointed out the inferioirty of Puerto Rican rums as compared with Cuban and the gross inferiority of Virgin Island rums. ...There are, it is true, some reasonably good Puerto Rican Rums, but none as good as the Cuban. <amy of the brands are not even fairly good and you can't make a good Daiquirí without good rum.[162]

DAIQUIRÍ (EMBURY VERSION)

1 part sugar syrup
2 parts lime juice
8 parts White Label Cuban Rum

---

161   "Taste the Difference Dry Rum Makes!", *The Milwaukee Journal*, 10 August 1956.

162   Embury, David Augustus, *The Fine Art of Mixing Drinks* (New York: Doubleday, 1948).

Shake vigorously with plenty of finely crushed ice and
strain into chilled cocktail glasses.[163]

Back to Havana for a moment, where
the Havana Club and Bacardí "free bars" were
lubricating thirsty American and European
tourists throughout the 1930s right along side
the city's now-legendary bars.

THE DAIQUIRÍ À LA 1930S HAVANA

Despite the confusion over the name
and the recipe in the US, Havana's cantineros
still served up a Daiquirí Naturel made with
readily available key limes. The 1936 Sloppy Joe's
Cocktails Manual featured both a Daiquirí and
a Santiago made with lime juice:

DAIQUIRÍ
(SLOPPY JOE VERSION)

1 teaspoonful sugar
1 part rum
Juice of a lime
Shake with cracked ice, and serve in a Manhattan
glass.[164]

---

163   Embury, David Augustus, *The Fine Art of Mixing Drinks* (New York:
Doubleday, 1948).

164   *Sloppy Joe's Cocktail Manual* (Havana: Sloppy Joe's, 1936)

SANTIAGO
(SLOPPY JOE VERSION)

1 Teaspoonful of sugar.
1 Part of Rum.
The juice of a lime.
Drops of grenadine.
Shake with cracked ice, and serve in Manhattan
glass.[165]

Emilio "Maragato" González was famed for his Daiquirís which he served around 1913 at the Hotel Plaza, according to Jaime Ariansen Cespedes which was probably made with lime or key lime juice.[166]

However, it was the version that La Florida's owner, Constantino Ribalaigua Vert, created—the Daiquirí Frappé (aka: Daiquirí No. 4)—that became the toast of the town and the entire world.

In the establishment's 1937 *Bar La Florida* book, United Press journalist Jack Cuddy immortalised Constante's Daiquirí No. 4:

Dos onzas de "Bacardi", que se agitan en una cotelera. Se agrega una cucharadita de azúcar granulada muy fina, para sumarle después otra de marrasquino, o sea, este cordial fabricado con cerezas silvestres de Dalmacia. Mézclese con todo

---

165   *Sloppy Joe's Cocktail Manual* (Havana: Sloppy Joe's, 1936)

166   "La Historia del Daiquirí: El Ciclón del Caribe", http://www. historiacocina.com/historia/articulos/Daiquirí.htm

el jugo de una media naranja lima. Y complétese la
medida con hielo muy fino, tan fino que esté casi
pulverizado. Coloqúese des- pués la cotelera en
una de esas batidoras eléctricas que tienen todos
los buenos bares, y en las que se) preparan los
chocolates y brebajes semejantes. Tres minutos allí.
Si no se dispone de batidora eléctrica, se usa una
cotelera corriente, pero entonces por un minuto
más. Se hielan los vasitos en que se vaya a tomar el
cocktail, y se sirve el Daiquiri Número 4.[167]

Cuddy mentions a medium *lima* [lime].
But the recipes that followed in the same book
dictated that Constante's five versions of the
Daiquirí used *limon verde* [green lemon] which
the English translator interpreted as lemon:

DAIQUIRI #1 (LA FLORIDA VERSION)

2 ounces Bacardí
1 teaspoon sugar
Juice of half a green lemon
Cracked ice.
Shake well and strain into a cocktail glass.[168]

DAIQUIRI #2 (LA FLORIDA VERSION)

2 ounces Bacardí
Several dashes curaçao

---

167   Vert, Constantino Ribalaigua, *Bar La Florida* (Havana: C. Ribalaigua y
Co, 1937).

168   Vert, Constantino Ribalaigua, *Bar La Florida* (Havana: C. Ribalaigua y
Co, 1937).

1 teaspoon Orange juice

1 teaspoon sugar

Juice of half a green lemon

Cracked ice.

Shake well and strain into a cocktail glass.[169]

DAIQUIRI #3 (LA FLORIDA VERSION)

2 ounces Bacardí

1 teaspoon Grapefruit juice

1 teaspoon Maraschino liqueur

1 teaspoon sugar

Juice of half a green lemon

Shake well and strain into a cocktail glass. Serve frappe.[170]

DAIQUIRI #4 (HOWARD AND MAE) (LA FLORIDA VERSION)

2 ounces Bacardí

1 teaspoon Maraschino liqueur

1 teaspoon sugar

Juice of half a green lemon

Mix in a blender with cracked ice. Serve frappe.[171]

169   Vert, Constantino Ribalaigua, *Bar La Florida* (Havana: C. Ribalaigua y Co, 1937).

170   Vert, Constantino Ribalaigua, *Bar La Florida* (Havana: C. Ribalaigua y Co, 1937).

171   Vert, Constantino Ribalaigua, *Bar La Florida* (Havana: C. Ribalaigua y Co, 1937).

DAIQUIRI #5 (PINK)
(LA FLORIDA VERSION)

2 ounces Bacardí

1 teaspoon Maraschino liqueur

1 teaspoon sugar

1 teaspoon grenadine syrup

Juice of half a green lemon

Mix in a blender with cracked ice. Serve frappe.[172]

What's interesting is that Constante's Bacardí Cocktail (Special) distinctly called for lemon and Angostura bitters instead of grenadine syrup.

BACARDÍ COCKTAIL (SPECIAL)
(LA FLORIDA VERSION)

2 ounces Bacardí

1 dash Angostura

½ teaspoon curaçao

Juice of half a lemon

½ teaspoon sugar

Shake and strain. [173]

We won't discuss the obvious facts about the El Floridita Daiquirís. Thanks to author Ernest Hemingway, this is the Daiquirí that had the longest legs. It resonated with the A-list

---

172   Vert, Constantino Ribalaigua, *Bar La Florida* (Havana: C. Ribalaigua y Co, 1937).

173   Vert, Constantino Ribalaigua, *Bar La Florida* (Havana: C. Ribalaigua y Co, 1937).

celebrity set, who were introduced to it by Hemingway, for the most part, until he left Cuba.

With little to no access to this "Cradle of the Daiquirí", what were Americans in the US being told was a true Daiquirí?

A CHANGE OF MARKETING TACTICS & HISTORY REWRITES ITSELF AGAIN

No one ever seemed to get the recipes for the Daiquirí and the Bacardí cocktails right. Even by 1960, two conflicting recipes for the Bacardí cocktail appear in the United Kingdom Bartenders Guide official drink guide—the book that was supposed to standardise recipes throughout its membership.

BACARDÍ (UKBG VERSION, IN ADVERTISEMENT)

Take the juice of half a lemon, add ½ teaspoonful of caster sugar and a measure of Bacardi White Label. Shake well with cracked ice. Strain and serve.[174]

---

174   *The U.K.B.G. Guide to Drinks, 3rd Edition. (Revised).* (London: United Kingdom Bartenders Guide, 1960).

BACARDÍ
(UKBG VERSION)

½ Glass Bacardi Rum.
Juice ½ lime.
1 teaspoon of Grenadine.
Shake and Strain.[175]

DAIQUIRÍ
(UKBG VERSION)

¾ Bacardi
¼ Fresh Lime or Lemon Juice.
3 Dashes Gomme Syrup.
Shake and Strain. [176]

By the 1970s the Bacardí company re-wrote the histories and the recipes of the Daiquirí and the Bacardí, once again. In its 1976 and 1979 editions of *The Bacardí Party Book* these drinks are seen in a new light:

BACARDÍ DAIQUIRÍ
(1970S VERSION)

(The original Daiquirí was made with Bacardí in 1896—and the best still are!)
Put 2 tsps of Minute Maid limeade or lemonade concentrate, or dry or liquid Daiquirí mix, in a shaker or pitcher with ice. Add generous jigger of Bacardí

---

175 *The U.K.B.G. Guide to Drinks, 3rd Edition. (Revised).* (London: United Kingdom Bartenders Guide, 1960).

176 *The U.K.B.G. Guide to Drinks, 3rd Edition. (Revised).* (London: United Kingdom Bartenders Guide, 1960).

light rum. Shake or stir well. Serve in a cocktail glass or on the rocks. (If you prefer fresh fruit, use juice of 1/2 lime or lemon with 1/2 tsp sugar.)[177]

FROZEN DAIQUIRÍ (1970S VERSION)

Follow Daiquirí recipe, using cracked ice and blending ingredients in electric blender for 10 to 20 seconds. May be served in cocktail glasses with short straws.[178]

BACARDÍ COCKTAIL (1970S VERSION)

Use Daiquirí recipe (page 2), add tsp of grenadine. Serve straight up in a cocktail glass or on the rocks. The Bacardí Cocktail is a little sweeter than a Daiquirí and has a beautiful pink cooler. (For your protection, the N.Y. Supreme Court ruled that a Bacardí Cocktail is not a Bacardí Cocktail unless it's made with Bacardí rum.)[179]

> In the end, there really was a difference between the Daiquirí and the Bacardí Cocktail. The grenadine really was part of the recipe after all!

---

177   *The Bacardi Party Book* (Miami: Bacardi, 1976 and 1979).

178   *The Bacardi Party Book* (Miami: Bacardi, 1976 and 1979).

179   *The Bacardi Party Book* (Miami: Bacardi, 1976 and 1979).

CONCLUSIONS ABOUT THE DAIQUIRÍ

There is more than one drink that was christened Daiquirí and there always has been. In many ways it is much like the story of the two Blackthorn Cocktails, one made with Irish whiskey, the other made with Sloe Gin.

It's also like the story of the two Mai Tais, a short drink created by Trader Vic Bergeron and a long drink created by Ernst Gantt of Don the Beachcomber.

A great name that resonates with consumers is hard to beat.

There are three drinks named the Daiquirí which are progressive, stylistic modifications to the British ponche and the Cuban Canchánchara formula of rum, citrus juice, sweetener, and dilution:

1. Jennings S Cox's Daiquirí that follows the classic Rum Sour recipe: rum, lemon juice, mineral water, and sugar.

2. Facundo Bacardí's Daiquirí: rum, lime juice, and sugar with the option to add grenadine syrup.

3. Constante Ribalaigua's Daiquirí #4 (aka: El Floridita Daiquirí): rum, lime juice, maraschino liqueur, and sugar.

Variations on these three recipes occur between 1900 and 1979 as the table at the end of this chapter illustrates.

When looking for the first Daiquirí, the question comes down to chronology. The Cox Daiquirí was the first Daiquirí recipe based on accounts from Pagliuchi. But the first Daiquirí recipe to appear in print was the 1914 Jacques Straub version.

This means that Bacardí's current public relations agency of record is not promoting the "original" Daiquirí. It was initially made with lemons, not limes nor key limes. Bacardí currently promotes this one yet does not include mineral water even though it is using the handwritten recipe as evidence. In truth, it is still promoting the 1935 Daiquirí Naturel that it could not attach to its name.

The Havana Club Special that was promoted by José Arechabala SA during the 1930s and 1940s was close to the original because it offered the option of using either lemon or lime juice, which the Bacardí company also promoted doing during the 1970s.

The Floridita Daiquirí made with lime juice or "green lemon juice" and the addition of maraschino liqueur became the most famous thanks to Ernest Hemingway and other American celebrities.

However, any of the versions that we have demonstrated in this report cannot be made with today's version of Bacardí, because by its own admission, the original is no longer made with Cuban rum. Since the 1950s, they have been promoting a Dry Daiquirí made with Puerto Rican rum.

So then, was the original Daiquirí made with Daiquirí Rum, which was available in the US until the late 1960s? We may never know.

A CHRONOLOGICAL TABLE OF DAIQUIRÍ RECIPES

YEAR	SOURCE	DRINK NAME	RECIPE
1734	Nouveau Dictionnaire de Sobrino, François, Espangol et Latin, Tome III	Ponche	aguardiente, agua, limon y azucar
1743	Transactions Philosophiques de la Société Royale de Londres pour le Mois de Février 1743	Ponche (aka: Diapente)	16 ounces water 1 ½ ounces sugar 2 ½ ounces fresh lemon juice 3 ½ ounces spirit
1870s	Spanish Wikipedia	Canchanchara	60 ml aguardiente 2 spoonfuls honey 1 teaspoon lemon juice Ice Mix well in a glass the honey and lime juice. Add aguardiente and ice. Stir.
1870s	El Floridita website	Canchanchara	2/3 rum 1/3 lemon juice

YEAR	SOURCE	DRINK NAME	RECIPE
UNK	Handwritten recipe "Original" "Mr Cox's"	Daiquirí	(for 6 persons) The juice of 6 lemons 6 teaspoons of sugar 6 Bacardí cups— "Carta Blanca" 2 small cups of mineral water Plenty of crushed ice Put all ingredients in a cocktail shaker and shake well. Do not strain as the glass may be served with some ice
1900	Harry Johnson's Bartenders Manual	Medford Rum Sour	(Use a large bar glass.) 1/2 tablespoonful of sugar; 3 or 4 dashes of lemon juice; 1 squirt of syphon selter, dissolved well 1 wine glass of Medford rum; Fill | of the glass with ice. Stir well with a spoon strain into a sour glass, ornament with fruit, etc., and serve. This is an old Boston drink, and has the reputation of being cooling and pleasant.

YEAR	SOURCE	DRINK NAME	RECIPE
1900	Harry Johnson's Bartenders Manual	Columbia Skin	1 teaspoonful sugar, dissolve with a little water; 1 slice of lemon; 2 or 3 pieces of broken ice; 1 wine glass of Medford rum; Stir up well with a spoon; grate a little nutmeg on top and serve. This drink is called Columbia Skin by the Boston people.
1909	Army Navy Club website	Army & Navy Club Daiquirí	A Glass, a jigger of rum, the juice of half a lime, a teaspoon of sugar, finely shaved ice and a good stir. No bitters!—and no better in town! Visit the lounge for a pre- or post dinner drink, or for an after work wind down
1914	Drinks by Jacques Straub	Daiguirí Cocktail	2/3 jigger lime juice 1/3 jigger rum 1 bar spoon powdered sugar Shake well with fine ice; strain into cocktail glass.
1914	Drinks by Jacques Straub	Bacardí Cocktail	½ pony grenadine syrup. 2/3 jigger Bacardi rum. juice of half a lime. Shake well. Strain. Serve.

YEAR	SOURCE	DRINK NAME	RECIPE
1915	Manuel del Cantinero	Daiquirí Cocktail	1 green lemon [read: lime], juiced 1 teaspoon granulated sugar 1 teaspoon grenadine 1 teaspoon curaçao 45 ml Ron Bacardí Shake and serve as a frappe in a Champagne coupe.
1916	Hugo R Ensslin	Cuban Cocktail	1 jigger Bacardí Rum 2 dashes Gum Syrup Juice of 1/2 Lime Shake well in a mixing glass with cracked ice, strain and serve.
1916	Hugo R Ensslin	Bacardí Cocktail	1 drink Bacardí Rum Juice of 1/2 Lime 2 dashes Gum Syrup Shake well in a mixing glass with cracked ice, strain and serve.
1916	Hugo R Ensslin	Daiguiri [sic] Cocktail	1 jigger Bacardí Rum 2 dashes Grenadine Syrup Juice of 1 Lime Shake well in a mixing glass with cracked ice, strain and serve in a cocktail glass.
1927	El Arte de Hacer un Cocktail y Algo Mas	Daiquirí	3 parts rum Juice of half a lemon 1 teaspoon sugar Shake and serve.

YEAR	SOURCE	DRINK NAME	RECIPE
1927	El Arte de Hacer un Cocktail y Algo Mas	Daiquirí Dulce	½ rum ½ lemon juice a little grenadine syrup Shake and serve.
1934	Havana Club compliment card	Havana Club Special	1 tsp sugar ½ oz lime or lemon juice 1 oz Havana Club Rum Dissolve lime juice and sugar first in the cocktail shaker. Add Havana Club Rum and cracked ice according to number of cocktails to be mixed. Shake this mixture until it is frozen.
1935	G Selmar Fougner	Daiquirí	½ oz lime juice 2 teaspoons sugar 1 ½ oz Bacardí Stir ingredients over ice and strain into a champagne glass packed with finely cracked ice.
1936	Sloppy Joe's Cocktail Manual	Daiquirí	1 teaspoonful sugar 1 part rum juice of a lime Shake with cracked ice, and serve in a Manhattan glass.
1936	Sloppy Joe's Cocktail Manual	Santiago	1 Teaspoonful of sugar. 1 Part of Rum. The juice of a lime. Drops of grenadine. Shake with cracked ice, and serve in Manhattan glass.

YEAR	SOURCE	DRINK NAME	RECIPE
1937	Café Royal Cocktail Book	Daiquirí	3 dashes Gomme Syrup. ¾ Daiquiri Rum. ¼ Juice of a Lime or Lemon. Shake.
1937	Facundo Bacardí in the Miami Herald	Original Daiquirí	60-90 ml Bacardí
1937	Facundo Bacardí in the Miami Herald	Daiquirí (Venus Hotel Bar)	The juice of half a large, or one small lime was squeezed into a shaker containing one teaspoonful of granulated sugar. Two ounces of Ron Bacardi (Carte Blanca) were added and a generous quantity of shaved ice prepared the shaker for frosting. When the mixture was thoroughly frapped it was then poured (not strained) into a chilled glass known as a "flute"
1937	Bar La Florida	Daiquirí No. 1	2 ounces Bacardí 1 teaspoon sugar Juice of half a green lemon Cracked ice. Shake well and strain into a cocktail glass.

YEAR	SOURCE	DRINK NAME	RECIPE
1937	Bar La Florida	Daiquirí No. 2	2 ounces Bacardí Several dashes curaçao 1 teaspoon Orange juice 1 teaspoon sugar Juice of half a green lemon Cracked ice. Shake well and strain into a cocktail glass.
1937	Bar La Florida	Daiquirí No. 3	2 ounces Bacardí 1 teaspoon Grapefruit juice 1 teaspoon Maraschino liqueur 1 teaspoon sugar Juice of half a green lemon Shake well and strain into a cocktail glass. Serve frappe.
1937	Bar La Florida	Daiquirí No. 4 (Howard and Mae)	2 ounces Bacardí 1 teaspoon Maraschino liqueur 1 teaspoon sugar Juice of half a green lemon Mix in a blender with cracked ice. Serve frappe.
1937	Bar La Florida	Daiquirí No. 5 (Pink)	2 ounces Bacardí 1 teaspoon Maraschino liqueur 1 teaspoon sugar 1 teaspoon grenadine syrup Juice of half a green lemon Mix in a blender with cracked ice. Serve frappe.

YEAR	SOURCE	DRINK NAME	RECIPE
1937	Bar La Florida	Bacardí Cocktail (Special)	2 ounces Bacardí 1 dash Angostura ½ teaspoon curaçao Juice of half a lemon ½ teaspoon sugar Shake and strain.
1939	The Gentlemen's Companion	Original Cuban DDaiquirí	1 whiskey glass (1 ½ oz) level full of Carta Blanca, or Carta de Oro Bacardi rum, 2 tsp of sugar, the juice of 1 ½ small green limes—strained; and very finely cracked ice.
1927	El Arte de Hacer un Cocktail y Algo Mas	Daiquirí Dulce	½ rum ½ lemon juice a little grenadine syrup Shake and serve.
1938	Schenley's Merry Mixer	Bacardí Cocktail	Juice of ½ green lime 1/2 teaspoon granulated sugar 1 jigger Bacardí White Label Shake well with finely shipped ice and pour into cocktail glass.
1946	The Stork Club Bar Book	Daiquirí	2 oz silver rum juice of half lime 1 tsp sugar Shake well and serve in 3 oz cocktail glass.

YEAR	SOURCE	DRINK NAME	RECIPE
1946	The Stork Club Bar Book	Frozen Daiquirí	2 oz silver rum juice of half lime 1 tsp sugar dash of maraschino shaved ice Use electric mixer. Serve unstrained in champagne glass with short straws.
1946	The Stork Club Bar Book	French Daiquiri (credited to Ernest Luthi)	½ oz lime juice 2/3 oz bacardi rum a little sugar dash of cassis few fresh mint leaves Shake well. Serve in a cocktail glass.
1948	El Arte del Cantinero	Daiquirí	1 shot Cuban rum 2 teaspoons sugar Juice of a medium-sized key lime [read: limon criollo]. Ice. Shake 25 times, strain, and serve. If the customer desires add 3 dashes of grenadine syrup.
1948	El Arte del Cantinero	Bacardí No. 1	1 teaspoon sugar 1 shot Bacardí Rum Juice of half a lemon Ice. Shake well, strain, and serve.
1948	El Arte del Cantinero	Bacardí No. 2	4 parts Bacardí Rum 1 part grenadine syrup 1 part lemon juice Ice. Shake 35 times, strain, and serve.

YEAR	SOURCE	DRINK NAME	RECIPE
1951	The Bartender's Manual (Jack Townsend)	Daiquirí	1 ½ oz rum juice of half lime 1 teaspoon sugar Shake well with ice. Strain into cocktail glass.
1951	The Bartender's Manual (Jack Townsend)	Santiago Cocktail	2 Dashes Grenadine 2 Dashes Lemon Juice 1 Glass Bacardi Rum Shake well and strain into cocktail glass.
1951	The Bartender's Manual (Jack Townsend)	Bacardí Cocktail	1 ½ oz rum juice of half lime 1 teaspoon sugar Shake well with ice. Strain into cocktail glass.
1956	Milwaukee Journal	Dry Daiquirí	1 ½ ounces Puerto Rican rum ½ ounce fresh lime juice Sugar to taste Then shake like the dickens with cracked ice.
1960	The U.K.B.G. Guide to Drinks	Bacardí Cocktail (ad in the book)	Take the juice of half a lemon, add ½ teaspoonful of caster sugar and a measure of Bacardi White Label. Shake well with cracked ice. Strain and serve.
1960	The U.K.B.G. Guide to Drinks	Bacardí Cocktail (in the book text)	½ Glass Bacardi Rum. Juice ½ lime. 1 teaspoon of Grenadine. Shake and Strain.

YEAR	SOURCE	DRINK NAME	RECIPE
1960	The U.K.B.G. Guide to Drinks	Daiquirí	¾ Bacardi ¼ Fresh Lime or Lemon Juice. 3 Dashes Gommer Syrup. Shake and Strain.
1976 and 1979	The Bacardí Party Book	Bacardí Daiquirí	(The original Daiquirí was made with Bacardí in 1896—and the best still are!) Put 2 tsps of Minute Maid limeade or lemonade concentrate, or dry or liquid Daiquirí mix, in a shaker or pitcher with ice. Add generous jigger of Bacardí light rum. Shake or stir well. Serve in a cocktail glass or on the rocks. (If you prefer fresh fruit, use juice of 1/2 lime or lemon with 1/2 tsp sugar.)
1976 and 1979	The Bacardí Party Book	Bacardí Cocktail	Use Daiquirí recipe (page 2), add tsp of grenadine. Serve straight up in a cocktail glass or on the rocks. The Bacardí Cocktail is a little sweeter than a Daiquirí and has a beautiful pink cooler. (For your protection, the N.Y. Supreme Court ruled that a Bacardí Cocktail is not a Bacardí Cocktail unless it's made with Bacardí rum.)

YEAR	SOURCE	DRINK NAME	RECIPE
1976 and 1979	The Bacardí Party Book	Frozen Daiquirí	Follow Daiquirí recipe, using cracked ice and blending ingredients in electric blender for 10 to 20 seconds. May be served in cocktail glasses with short straws.

Chapter 14
★ ★ ★ ★

Mojito:
The "Authentically" Cuban Drink

A Cuban icon that is as popular (if not more so) as Brazil's national drink, the Caipirinha, the Mojito is reputed to be one of the world's first mixed drinks. It proudly stands along the Mint Julep, which boasts an ancestry that spans from a sweetened medicinal preparation made by Arab physicians to an anti-malarial sipped by the French to a simple British stomach remedy.

In the 1753 edition of *The New Dispensatory*, a simple Stomach Julep called for six ounces of "simple mint water" (which the book later describes as a distillation of 1.5 pounds of dry mint leaves and water), two drams of saffron syrup, and two ounces of spirituous mint water made by distilling 1.5 pounds of dry mint leaves and 1 gallon of spirit.[180]

JULEPUM STOMACHICUM

180 ml "simple mint water" (distilled mint water)
5 ml saffron syrup, and two ounces of
60 ml spirituous mint water
Blend together and serve. [181]

The reason that we mention this considerably earlier recipe for a Mint Julep is that it defends an assumption that British sailors and pirates may have known that mint is an excellent remedy for stomach disorders as far back as the Elizabethan times.

Why do we start with a discussion about Mint Juleps? Because it offers a new in-

---

180   Lewis, William. *The New Dispensatory...Intended as a Correction, and Improvement of [John] Quincy* (London: J. Nourse, 1753).

181   Lewis, William. *The New Dispensatory...Intended as a Correction, and Improvement of [John] Quincy* (London: J. Nourse, 1753).

sight into the origins of the Mojito's purported ancestor the Draque.

THE DRAQUE:
A PIRATE'S BEST REMEDY

In his seminal 1981 book *El Hijo Alegre de la Caña de Azúcar*, Fernando G Campoamor offered in his glossary a key insight into the popularity, during the 1800s, of the "Draque", the alleged ancestor of the Mojito.[182]

The author pointed to Sir Francis Drake as the drink's inventor. In recent times, that designation has been handed Richard Drake who allegedly was at sea with the famed privateer and crafted the drink to honour (or aid) his commander. But was he?

First cousin to Sir Francis Drake, Richard Drake of Esher, was the son of John and Anne (Grenville) Drake and first cousin of the navigator Sir Francis Drake. Yes. He did work with his cousin, taking charge of the Spanish Armada prisoners taken off Plymouth, in 1588, which included the Spanish vice-admiral, Don Pedro de Valdés, whom he kept at his manor of Esher in Surrey, pending arrangements for

182   Diaz, Fernando González Campoamor. *El hijo alegre de la caña de azúcar* (Havana: Editorial Científico- técnica, 1981).

the ransom. But he never went to sea with his cousin.

However, Francis Drake's nephew did.

Admiral Sir Richard Hawkins was the son of Admiral Sir John Hawkins and Sir Francis Drake's nephew. He was also a well-known "Sea Dog" or British privateer. In 1582 he accompanied his uncle, Sir Francis Drake, on an early voyage to raid the Brazilian coast. Three years later, he captained one of the galliots in Drake's fleet that scoured the Spanish Main from the Caribbean to the Gulf of Mexico.

In Irene Wright's 1932 translation of both Spanish and British accounts of Sir Francis Drake's escapades titled, *Documents Concerning the English Voyages to the Spanish Main*, a tale of this voyage on folds. In 1586, Drake's fleet devastated both the ports of Santo Domingo and Cartegna in his quest for Spanish booty. He intended to raid one more port—Havana. But crews on all of his ships fell ill and he postponed his plan.[183]

Dr Eugene Lyon, Flagler College Center for Historic Research, in 1996, translated at historian Jerry Wilkinson's request an interesting document on a search for Drake at the Keys.

---

183   Wright, Irene Aloha. *Documents concerning English voyages to the Spanish Main, 1569-1580 : I, Spanish documents selected from the Archives of the Indies at Seville; II, English accounts, "Sir Francis Drake revived" and others, reprinted* (London: Hakluyt Society, 1932)

A letter by Alonso Suarez de Toledo to the Spanish Crown, written at Havana, 27 June 1586, on the appearance and disappearance of Sir Francis Drake:

...the rest of the [English] fleet passed by the harbour, to the east. They anchored three leagues (10 miles) away, at Guacuranao River, the ships close-hauled, and remained there that night. Next day, toward evening all the pinnaces [28'-32' open boats] sailed near this port. It was believed that they would land men and certainly it was hoped that they would, for had they done so, not a man would have returned aboard. They would have paid here for what they have done, and for their evil heretical lives. . . On June 4th the Englishman disappeared. On the 5th...two frigates were hastily sent out, each carrying twenty musketeers. One went toward Las Tortugas, to see if the enemy had retraced his course, and the other toward the mouth of the channel with an interpreter to learn of the Indians whether they had seen him [Drake] pass. Both vessels returned and from the Indians it was understood that the enemy had gone.

Was it during this "lost" period that Richard Hawkins offered his uncle some relief from the illness that befell him and most of the fleet's crew?

Few British vessels left port—official naval or privateer ship—without a few essential medical supplies. Surely enough reports had returned to Britain about the dangers of tropical stomach disorders, malaria, yellow fever, and other ailments in the Caribbean.

A Stomach Julep made with mint was probably among them. Or was Hawkins clever enough to concoct a quick remedy from *aguardiente* and a local mint called *hierbabuena*, which some say was *mentha sativa* or whorled mint (which the natives chewed for stomach relief) and others claim was *mentha suaveolens* or woolly mint (aka: Cuban mint), sweetened with a little sugar to make the medicine go down more pleasantly?

785. Mentha sativa L.
Whorled Mint ; Li.

Based on the distinctive red stem that we noticed in the mint used to make Mojitos throughout Havana and the tradition surrounding the use of *mentha sativa* as a digestive remedy, we determined that variety, not *mentha suaveolens* is the true *hierbabuena*.

There is little doubt that Drake's fleet appropriated some form of *aguardiente de caña* at every Caribbean port that it raided. Even before the rum ration was established among the British Royal Navy in 1655, there was a reason for sailors to acquire some form of spirit before heading out to sea. Five years earlier, British Admiral Robert Blake substituted a pint-per day brandy ration for his sailors' gallon-per-day beer ration because it saved valuable storage. Surely Drake had discovered a similar strategy during his earlier voyages to the Caribbean.

In those days, fresh water was acquired at a premium. Seawater could be distilled, but the process was slow and required too much fuel to execute. If a fresh water supply was found on an island or along a coastline, it was taken on board in casks and stored. In these vessels, water quickly stagnated and developed algae. To make this liquid palatable, beer or wine was added. In Drake's case, *aguardiente* would have been the ready solution.

Or was this remedy introduced to both Hawkins and Drake by the French corsairs and *cimarrones* (aka: Maroons) who were escaped slaves from Caribbean sugar plantations? Maybe the type of mint employed was known to the *cimarrones* who had learnt it from the locals. But the spirits-based recipe shows the earmarks of European birth.

Revived and refreshed, Drake and his fleet plundered one more city—St Augustine FL—before they sailed north to rescue members of the first colony at Roanoke VA. He returned a hero.

With a price on his head of 20,000 ducats (about £4 million) offered by King Philip II of Spain, Drake was best known as the "Dragon"—El Draque. So it would not be surprising that the legend about his recovery from illness with a spirited mint concoction spread throughout the Spanish Main.

As Campoamor further noted, according to a dictionary of Spanish slang that was assembled in the late 1800s by Venezuelan physician, historian, and linguist Lisandro Alvardo, the word *draque* is also associated with an *aguardiente*-based stomach remedy in Maracaibo, Venezuela (another port that Drake attacked). An "energetic herbal tisane" called *drague* also appeared in Mexico. The same drink offered relief from dehydration in Cartagena, Colombia (another Drake target). [184]

Even after Drake's death from dysentery, in 1596, after an unsuccessful attack on San Juan, Puerto Rico, his namesake potion lived on as the *draque*, *drague*, *draquecito*, *drak*, or *drac*.

---

184   Diaz, Fernando González Campoamor. *El hijo alegre de la caña de azúcar* (Havana: Editorial Científico- técnica, 1981).

Campoamor stated that the name and the drink's two main ingredients make an appearance in Ramón de Palma y Romay's 1838 novella *El Cólera en La Habana en 1833* in which a character remarks:

> Yo me tomo todos los días a las once un draquecito de aguardiente de caña con azúcar y me va perfectamente [Every day at eleven o'clock I take my *draquecito* of aguardiente de caña with sugar and it suits me perfectly.][185]

DRAQUECITO

Aguardiente
Sugar
Combine ingredients and serve.

Once again, someone seeks relief (or prevention) from the symptoms of cholera that include stomach distress and dehydration. But in this statement there is no indication that mint or limes were part of the recipe.

We do believe that mint was an integral part of the Draquecito despite this omission simply because Caribbean natives knew that this plant was an excellent digestive remedy. However, we question whether limes were part of

185   Diaz, Fernando González Campoamor. *El hijo alegre de la caña de azúcar* (Havana: Editorial Científico- técnica, 1981).

192 ★ ★ ★ ★ ★ ★ ★ CUBAN COCKTAILS

the Draque concoction. They were not a known remedy for scurvy in Drake's day. This citrus—or lemons—may have been added at a later date as drinks such as the 1600s British Punch, Bajan Rum Punch from Barbados, Ti Punch in Martinique and other French-Caribbean colonies and 1800s Canchánchara in Cuba were born.

However, Fernando Ortiz in his 1940 book *Contrapunteo Cubano del Tabaco y el Azucar* quotes an article titled "La Boca del Moro" written by journalist and theatre manager Federico Villoch in the 28 October 1940 edition of *Diario de la Marina* that claims the limes and mint were always part of the equation:[186]

A good dose of aguardiente de caña, half a glass, with sugar, a little water, intoned with a few sprigs of hierba buena and a wedge of lime. It was consumed as the draque until 1800 and its peak until it was displaced by Cuban rum and Holland gin.[187]

Since the original Villoch article has not been located, it is difficult to determine if the journalist went on to say that "When aguardiente is replaced with rum, the Draque is to be called a Mojito."

186   Ortiz, Fernando. *Contrapunteo Cubano del Tabaco y el Azucar* (Havana: J. Montero, 1940).

187   Villoch, Federico. "Diario lde la Marina", *La Boca del Moro*, 28 October 1940.

This version of Villoch's statement has been circulated on the internet since 2006, when it appeared in a *Miami Herald* entry posted on 28 June 2006. Since then it has been picked up by numerous drinks blogs and even *Diffords-Guide* includes it in its entry on the Mojito #1.

Gin? Yes, there was a gin-based Mojito. A recipe for this drink can be found in the 1935 *Bar La Florida*.

THE PROGRESSION FROM DRAQUECITO TO MOJITO

So when did the Draquecito evolve into the Mojito?

According to journalist Ciro Bianchi Ross, as related by Cuban historian Miguel Bonera, the term "Mojito Batido" first appeared in print in 1910.[188]

But there is no mention as to the source of this information. Was it an article that Bianchi Ross wrote or an item that he referenced from 1910?

In a more recent document, Bonera narrates that the Mojito itself was born at La Concha in Havana:

188　Bonera Miranda, Miguel, *Oro Blanco : Una Historia Empresarial de Ron Cubano, Tomo 1*, (Toronto: Libros Latinamerica Inc, 2000).

In the Bar of the Hotel-Balneario "La Concha", in
Havana, a bar attendant called Rogelio created, in
1910, a combination of white Cuban rum, ice, pomelo
or lemon juice, unrefined sugar, a few dashes of
Angostura bitters and soda water which was baptized
with the name of 'Mojito'. Some of them, later, tried to
affirm that: '… it was born in the 1930s in the Sevilla
Hotel, in Havana, by someone looking for a drink that
was symbolized Cuba.'

LA CONCHA MOJITO

Cuban rum
Pomelo or lemon juice
Unrefined sugar
Angostura bitters
Soda water

It is possible that the people he mentioned who "tried to affirm that: 'it was born
in the 1930s in the Sevilla Hotel…'" were the
same individuals who asserted that nearly every
popular drink made in Havana was invented by
Eddie Woelke while he was behind the bar at
the Sevilla-Biltmore Hotel.

Author Rafael Lam narrates a little
more about La Concha that:

In this club on Marianao beach, the demand for
Mojitos was so great, that sometimes the bar would
run out of lemons. Bartenders would them use

pomelo juice instead. This variation was considered to be higher class and thus costlier.[189]

In effect, La Concha Mojito is a Rum Rickey, a style of mixed drinks that appeared in Washington DC in 1883 and became a nationwide hit when the Gin Rickey was introduced at the 1893 Columbian Exposition in Chicago. Made with the juice and shell of half a lime and optional bitters (unlike its British ancestor, the Collins, which was made with lemon juice and optional bitters), the basic Rickey recipe is a prime example:

WHISKEY RICKEY

(Use a medium size fizz glass.)
1 or 2 pieces of ice;
Squeeze the juice of 1 good-sized lime or 2 small ones;
1 wine-glass of rye whiskey
Fill up the glass with club soda, selters, or vichy; and serve with a spoon.[190]

Two similar recipes made their way overseas to the UK by the 1930s and were included in the 1937 *Café Royal Cocktail Book*: The Daiquirí Sour and the Daiquirí Fizz.

---

189   Lam, Rafael. *La Bodeguita del Medio* (Havana: Editorial José Martí, 1994).

190   Johnson, Harry, *The Bartenders' Manual, Revised Edition* (New York: Harry Johnson, 1900).

DAIQUIRÍ SOUR (1937 VERSION)

Juice of ½ Lemon
1 teaspoon superfine sugar
1 glass Daiquirí Rum
Shake. Use champagne glass, add slice of orange
and a cherry. Fill with soda water.[191]

DAIQUIRÍ FIZZ (1937 VERSION)

Juice of ½ Lemon or Lime
1 teaspoon superfine sugar
½ Daiquirí Rum
Shake and strain into tumbler, fill with soda water.[192]

> In the 1927 book *El Arte de Hacer un Cocktail y Algo Mas*, another drink named the Mojo Criollo makes an appearance:

MOJO CRIOLLO (1927 VERSION)

Glass of rum
Drops of lemon juice
Spoonful of sugar
Serve in a medium glass with ice and a spoon.[193]

---

191   Tarling, William J. *Café Royal Cocktail Book* (London: Pall Mall, Ltd, 1937; Cheltenham: Mixellany Limited, 2009).

192   Tarling, William J. *Café Royal Cocktail Book* (London: Pall Mall, Ltd, 1937; Cheltenham: Mixellany Limited, 2009).

193   *El Arte de Hacer un Cocktail y Algo Mas* (Havana: Compañia Cervecera International SA, 1927; Cheltenham: Mixellany Limited, 2011)

And in another section, a Ron Rickey
and a Rum Rickey also make an appearance. [194]
Still no mint. Where's the mint!

THE MINT FINDS ITS WAY BACK INTO THE MOJITO

In John B Escalante's 1915 *Manuel del
Cantinero* a Mint Julep and a Ron Bacardí Julep
are about as close as it gets to marrying rum and
mint together in the same glass.

RON BACARDÍ JULEP (1915 VERSION)

Proceed as with the "Mint Julep" employing rum in
place of Cognac.[195]

However, in the 1935 edition of the *Bar
La Florida* cocktail book, all of the ingredients
come together in both a rum version made with
Martí Rum and a gin version:

MOJITO CRIOLLO (1935 VERSION)

Use an 8-ounce glass
Cracked ice
Several sprigs of hierbabuena

---

194   *El Arte de Hacer un Cocktail y Algo Mas* (Havana: Compañia Cervecera
International SA, 1927; Cheltenham: Mixellany Limited, 2011)

195   Escalante, John B. *Manuel del Cantinero* (Havana: Imprénta Moderna,
1915).

1 lemon peel, squeezing juice into glass
1 teaspoon sugar
2 ounces Martí Rum
Stir with spoon. Add sparkling water and serve
without straining.[196]
[EDITOR'S NOTE: It is assumed that the recipe calls
for the lemon shell to be tossed into the glass.]

> In a post-1937 edition, the recipe
> changed to use Bacardí instead of Martí rum.

MOJITO CRIOLLO (1937 VERSION)

Use an 8-ounce glass.
Cracked ice.
Several sprigs of Peppermint.
1 Lemon Peel, squeezing juice into glass.
1 Teaspoonful Sugar
2 ounces Bacardi
Stir with spoon
Add sparkling water Canada Dry and serve without
straining.[197]

> Similarly, in the 1936 edition of *Sloppy
> Joe's Cocktails Manual*, the Mojito calls for both
> mint plus the lime juice and shell.

MOJITO (1936 VERSION)

1 teaspoon sugar
One half a lime
1 part rum

---

196   *Bar La Florida* (Havana: La Florida, 1935).

197   *Bar La Florida* (Havana: La Florida, 1939).

Seltzer Water

Leaves of mint

Shell of the juiced lime

Serve in a highball glass with cracked ice.[198]

Over in Britain, the Mojito was included in the Supplementary List of drinks whose recipes are not provided in the 1937 *Café Royal Cocktail Book*. In the section's introduction the reader is invited to write to the United Kingdom Bartenders Guild for a copy of the recipe at a cost of 1 shilling per recipe.

By the time Angel Martinez bought out the Bodega La Complaciente on Calle Empedrado, in 1942, and renamed it Casa Martinez, the Mojito in its most familiar form had already evolved, a descendant of the Rum Rickey with the added aroma of mint; born from hands of a bartender at the La Concha Bar, 40 years earlier, and modified to suit local palates.

By the time he officially "inaugurated" La Bodeguita del Medio on 26 April 1950, he was already well known amongst Havana literati and avant-garde for his version of the drink, thanks to editor Felito Ayon and Ernest Hemingway.

But what of muddling the mint in the drink? Based on a description narrated by Hector Zumbado that was excerpted from *Prosas en Ajiaco* and reprinted in Lam's *La Bodeguita del*

Medio, it appears that La Bodeguita's cantineros started that trend. But the lime was squeezed into the glass—not muddled, which imparts too much bitterness into the drink. [199]

Some modern bartenders make the mistake of muddling the mint with lime wedges instead of squeezing in the juice and then dropping in the shell. Additionally, muddling the mint instead of "spanking" it to release the volatile oils does cause the mint to go chalky on the palate.

CONCLUSIONS ABOUT THE MOJITO

Let's start with the origins of the word "mojito" which Campoamor cites as a diminutive of the term "mojo". In his version, he states that it derives from the sauce that is made in the Canary Islands by the same name. [200]

We cannot justify this claim. The sauce—which contains garlic, cumin, coriander, chili, avocado, and lemon juice—has little to nothing to do with the cooler made with rum, lime or lemon juice, and in later recipes, mint.

Based on an assertion that the term is of African origin does lead us to believe that

---

199   Lam, Rafael. *La Bodeguita del Medio* (Havana: Editorial José Martí, 1994).

200   Diaz, Fernando González Campoamor. *El hijo alegre de la caña de azúcar* (Havana: Editorial Científico- técnica, 1981).

this diminutive is born from the term "mojo" that refers to a type of magical charm used in hoodoo and Santeria rituals. The mojo "spell" consists of a drawstring bag that is filled with herbs, spices, minerals, an incantation, and other objects that is used to invoke luck, attract love, money, induce confidence, or ward off demons and enemies.

A drink that made you feel good could be magical in that respect and would be christened with an endearment such as "dear little spell" in a culture that embraces Santeria such as Cuban culture.

As with the case of the Daiquirí, we believe that there are two Mojitos. One is based on the Rum Rickey. The other is a variation on a Mint Julep. The two recipes came together during the 1930s at Sloppy Joe's and at El Floridita (Bar La Florida).

Either of these establishments would have been the first to produce the drink that was ultimately popularised, during the 1950s, by Angel Martinez at La Bodeguita del Medio.

A survey of Sloppy Joe's drinks menus from 1918 through 1936 would best determine when he first started serving the Mojito. Similarly, a survey of La Florida's menus from 1900 through 1936 would determine when the establishment started serving a Mojito Criollo.

Based on the Sloppy Joe's and El Floridita recipes, Angel Martinez's was the first to muddle the mint according to the Mint Julep fashion.

What of the La Concha recipe? The La Concha Mojito was an exception to the rule that became the standard for making a Mojito, so should be considered as a separate and unique recipe on its own. Since we cannot find a copy of any material that proves up the La Concha Mojito recipe from 1910, we cannot verify that it is an authentic recipe.

One thing is certain. The Mojito is an authentic "born in Cuba" mixed drink.

A CHRONOLOGICAL TABLE OF MOJITO RECIPES

YEAR	SOURCE	DRINK NAME	RECIPE
1586	Unknown	Draque	aguardiente de cana honey or sugar hierbabuena combine ingredients and serve.
1753	The New Dispensatory	Julepum Stomachicum	180 ml "simple mint water" (distilled mint water) 5 ml saffron syrup, and two ounces of 60 ml spirituous mint water Blend together and serve.
1838	El colera en Habana	Draquecito	Aguardiente Sugar Combine ingredients and serve.
1900	Harry Johnson's Bartenders' Manual	Whiskey Rickey	(Use a medium size fizz glass.) 1 or 2 pieces of ice; Squeeze the juice of 1 good-sized lime or 2 small ones; 1 wine-glass of rye whiskey Fill up the glass with club soda, selters, or vichy; and serve with a spoon.
1910	Miguel Bonera and Rafael Lam	La Concha Mojito	Cuban rum Pomelo or lemon juice Unrefined sugar Angostura bitters Soda water

YEAR	SOURCE	DRINK NAME	RECIPE
1915	Manuel del Cantinero	Ron Bacardí Julep	Proceed as with the "Mint Julep" employing rum in place of Cognac.
1927	El Arte de Hacer un Cocktail y Algo Mas	Mojo Criollo	Glass of rum Drops of lemon juice Spoonful of sugar Serve in a medium glass with ice and a spoon.
1935	Bar La Flordia	Mojito Criollo	Use an 8-ounce glass Cracked ice Several sprigs of hierbabuena 1 lemon peel, squeezing juice into glass 1 teaspoon sugar 2 ounces Marti Rum Stir with spoon. Add sparkling water and serve without straining.
1935	Bar La Flordia	Mojito Crillio No. 2	Use an 8-ounce glass. Cracked ice. Several sprigs of Peppermint. 1 Lemon Peel, squeezing juice into glass. 1 Teaspoonful Sugar 2 ounces Bacardi Stir with spoon Add sparkling water Canada Dry and serve without straining.

YEAR	SOURCE	DRINK NAME	RECIPE
1936	Sloppy Joe's Cocktails Manual	Mojito	1 teaspoon sugar One half a lime 1 part rum Seltzer Water Leaves of mint Shell of the juiced lime Serve in a highball glass with cracked ice.
1937	Café Royal Cocktail Book	Daiquirí Sour	Juice of ½ Lemon 1 teaspoon superfine sugar 1 glass Daiquirí Rum Shake. Use champagne glass, add slice of orange and a cherry. Fill with soda water.
1937	Café Royal Cocktail Book	Daiquirí Fizz	Juice of ½ Lemon or Lime 1 teaspoon superfine sugar ½ Daiquirí Rum Shake and strain into tumbler, fill with soda water.

Chapter 15
★ ★ ★ ★

Piña Colada:
Born in Havana

James Bond never ordered one. It is hard to picture Ernest Hemingway setting a frosty one down next to his typewriter. Yet the Piña Colada is the drink of choice for countless cruise ship passengers, sun burnt tourists sporting loud Hawaiian shirts, countless infrequent imbibers, and, in truth, the one of the most broadly influential cocktails ever created.

Of course, like many great flavour combinations, before the drink's history began, the Piña Colada had an extensive prehistory.

Literally translated, Piña Colada means "strained pineapple". Minus the coconut, the combination of rum and pineapple dates back centuries.

The first record of Europeans encountering a pineapple points to the island of Guadeloupe—November 1493. Sailors on Christopher Columbus' second voyage named the curious fruit "*piña*" as it resembled a giant pinecone. The native Tainos were already drinking pineapple juice (which they called *yayamaby*) for refreshment and as a digestive aid, especially after consuming meat. Taino women were known to use it as an exfoliant and skin whitener. It was Columbus who brought the first pineapples to Spain. And this exotic fruit enchanted Europe.

It was not long before the pineapple became a symbol of wealth and hospitality throughout Europe and the colonies. Ship captains would mark a triumphant return from the tropics by placing a pineapple at their front gate: a gesture adopted from Caribbean tribes. Plus, the pineapple became the crowning glory on many upper-class European tables.

PINEAPPLE RUM

Wherever colonial rum and pineapple production took hold, the maceration of the two ingredients soon followed. For example, a traditional digestif in La Reunion, Rhums Arrangés Ananas macerates fresh pineapple, vanilla pods, and cinnamon with white La Reunion rhum.

The same held true for any country that had colonies where rum and pineapple were exported back to the homeland. With Barbados and Jamaica as likely initial sources, Britons went wild for Pineapple Rum.

An advertisement appeared in the 26 March 1783 edition of London's *Morning Herald And Daily Advertiser*. Bridge's on the Strand produced and sold Pineapple Rum for 16 shillings per gallon that was "so much approved for its flavour".

OLD BOTTLED RED PORT, at BRIDGES's, No. 445, Strand, oppofite Buckingham-ftreet. The Nobility and Gentry that are curious in the above article, may be fupplied with any quantity, two years in the bottle, at 23s. per doz. three ditto, at 26s. per doz. alfo fome that has been bottled four years, the fineft wine in this kingdom, at 28s. per doz. the bottles finely ftained with age; his old and not to be equalled SHERRY and MADEIRA, at 32s, and 42s. per doz. CALCAVALLA and MOUNTAIN, 10 years old, at 26s. per doz. fine rich TENT, 38s. per doz. alfo his PINE-APPLE RUM, (fo much approved for its delicious flavor) 16s. per gallon; and ten years old JAMAICA RUM and CONIAC FRENCH BRANDY, from 10s. to 14s. per gal. For ready money only, delivered to any part of the Town.
N. B. The above Wines are, upon oath, free from the vile practice of adulteration.

Six years later, the company changed hands and was renamed Glanfield's Vaults. But instead of selling simply Pineapple Rum, the new merchant sold the same product, alleging that it was aged for eleven years.

To the NOBILITY and GENTRY.

THE following genuine Wines, &c. now selling at the reduced prices, for ready money only, at
GLANFIELD's VAULTS, No. 445, Strand:

Burgundy of the firft growth,	—	3l. per doz.
Claret, ditto,	— —	45s. per doz.
Madeira, that has lain in the E. Indies 3 yrs.		44s. per doz.
Sherry, which has been round the W. Indies,		27s. per doz.
Five years bottled port,	—	23 per doz.
Red and white Port, vintage 1783,		21 per doz.
Calcavella, twelve years old,	—	23 per dez.
Lisbon, ten years old,	—	21 per doz.
Mountain, twelve years old,	—	22 per doz.
Pine-apple Rum, eleven years old,		11 per gall.
Fine old Jamaica, nine years old,		9 per gall.
Some Ditto, five years old,		8 per gall.
Real Coniac Brandy, ten years old,		10 per gall.
Some Ditto, four years old,	—	8 per gall.
Best Holland's Geneva,	—	9 per gall.
Some ditto,	— — —	8 per gall.
Fine Orange Shrub,	— —	9 per gall.

The Public may be affured with truth, that the above
Wines are of the very firft quality, being felected from
the moft choice vintages, and that there is no better
Wine to be had in this kingdom.

N. B. Bottles to be returned, or paid for on delivery.

Historian Samuel Morewood, in 1824,
wrote that:

The richness of flavour peculiar to this spirit, which
has rendered it famous in almost all part of the world,
is supposed to be derived from the raw juice and
the fragments of the sugar-cane, which are mashed
and fermented with other materials in the tun. The

essential oil of the cane is thus imparted to the wash, and carried over in the distillation; for sugar when distilled by itself has no peculiar flavour different from other spirits. Time adds much to the mildness and value of rum, which the planters, it is said, often improve by the addition of pineapple juice.[201]

By this time, Pineapple Rum was also very popular in parts of Europe, where fresh pineapple was far too costly for all but the wealthy. Even author Charles Dickens, in 1838, made mention of a hot version:

Mr. Stiggins was easily prevailed on to take another glass of the hot pineapple rum and water, and a second, and a third, and then to refresh himself with a slight supper previous to beginning again.[202]

The recipe was simple as given, in 1819, to housewives to make ample stock for their home:

An excellent flavour may be given to it by putting into the cask some pineapple rinds. The longer rum is kept, the more valuable it becomes. If your rum wants a head, whisk some clarified honey with a little

201   Morewood, Samuel. A*n Essay on the Inventions and Customs of both Ancients and Moderns in the Use of Inebriating Liquors* (London: Longman, Hurst, Rees, Orme, Brown, and Green, 1824).

202   Dickens, Charles. *The Posthumous Papers of the Pickwick Club* (London: Chapman & Hall, 1838-1839, 1842).

of the liquor, and pour the whole into the cask. Three
pounds of honey is sufficient for sixty gallons.

…

Rum…An excellent flavour may be given to it
by putting into the cask some pineapple rinds.
The longer the rum is kept the more valuable it
becomes.[203]

PIÑA CON RON

Piña con Ron is a familiar dessert in
Spanish homes. Sticks of peeled pineapple are
sautéed until golden in a little oil. Removed from
the heat, rum is pour over, deglazing the pan
and creating a rich sauce.

In the Caribbean, Jugo de Piña con Ron
or simply Piña con Ron—pineapple juice with
rum—was the perfect afternoon cooler.

Jugo de Piña was also called Piña Fria or
Piña Fria Colada, by the early 1800s, especially
after Cuban officials commissioned importation
ice from Spain and then from New England.
The first shipment from Boston arrived, in 1807,
thanks to Frederic Tudor.

Once ice manufacturing equipment was
developed and adopted on the island during

---

203   Hammond, Elizabeth. *Modern Domestic Cookery, and Useful Receipt Book*
(London: Dean & Munday, 1819).

the mid-1800s, ice cold pineapple juice with or without rum could be found from Santiago de Cuba in the east to Havana in the west.

When tourism exploded after the 1898 Spanish-American War, flocks of tourists joined the Caribbean planters and foreign businessmen in sipping frosty glasses of Piña con Ron. And American newspapers spread the word about this tropical treat.

ENTER THE CUBAN PIÑA COLADA

However, the US publication, *Travel* magazine, added a new twist when it mentioned another drink—Piña Colada.

At the end of almost every bar is a heap of ripe pineapples and green coconuts. An excellent drink is made by mixing the milk of the latter with a little gin and a tanal, a cake of sugar foam. But best of all is a piña colada, the juice of a perfectly ripe pineapple—a delicious drink in itself—rapidly shaken up with ice, sugar, lime and Bacardí rum in delicate proportions. What could be more luscious, more mellow and more fragrant?[204]

---

204   Brown, Irving. "Cuba's Vivacious Metropolis", *Travel Magazine*, December 1922.

There seemed to be some confusion during American Prohibition about the Piña Colada. Was it a non-alcoholic beverage— Piña Fria Colada—whose name was shortened to Piña Colada, simply because most Americans didn't understand Latin American Spanish? Or was it a mixed alcoholic drink as Irving Brown described?

The appeal for pineapple in the American palate was due largely in part to Jim Dole, who in 1901, founded the Hawaiian Pineapple Company, which strove to put the fruit in every American grocery store. So the Piña Colada or any pineapple drink was of interest to anyone in mainland America who had experienced the tropical fruit.

In the American media, some writers offered a temperate view of Cuba's delightful pineapple beverages. For example, author Harry La Tourette Foster, in his 1928 travelogue, wrote that:

> For the tea-totaler, there are plenty of non-alcoholic drinks obtainable in most places. In Havana, for instance, a favourite iced drink is jugo de piña or piña colada…[205]

---

205   Foster, Harry La Tourette, *The Caribbean Cruise* (New York: Dodd, Mead & Company, 1928).

A *Hartford Courant* reporter similarly stressed the Piña Colada's "non-alcoholic" nature:

> Down in Havana, Cuba, there is a soft drink that is very caressing to the esophagus, known in Spanish as either pina fria colada or piña fria sin colada, which might be copied in the United States where soft drinks are now legion.[206]

The reporter then devoted four paragraphs explaining how to order Piña Fria, Piña Colada, and Piña sin Colada from a Cuban café "bartender".

But it does leave one to wonder if this was just politically-correct editing. One *National Geographic Magazine* article mentioned the Piña Colada as non-alcoholic in one paragraph and later alludes to its potentially alcoholic nature:

> For the thirsty there is the "pineapple refreshment," made of freshly crushed pineapple, sugar, and water. Some order it colada, which means strained; others like food and drink together, and order it sin colar (without straining), with the pieces of crushed pineapple in the glass, a real treat.
>
> ...
>
> In the evening the cafés are busy places. Many of them, continental style, spread out over the sidewalk.

---

206 "Traveler Ecstatic over Cuban Drink" *The Hartford Courant*, 20 August 1922.

There the people sit, sip their drinks, smoke talk, and
watch the passers-by with thorough enjoyment. One
practically never sees an intoxicated Cuban, despite
the fact that they drink much wine and beer.

The poor people are the most patient and law-abiding
I have ever know. I have sat at a sidewalk café table,
surrounded by well-dressed, well-fed people, sipping
a piña colada (see text, page 365), and listening to an
orchestra of flashing-eyed beauties play and sing their
native music with its strange, yearning rhythm.[207]

Historical accounts tell us that when the
bodega La Piña de Plata [The Silver Pineapple]
opened in Havana, in 1820, it sold fresh juices.
Its speciality was pineapple juice. Beverage sales
were so successful that, in 1867, the establishment installed a restaurant and a bar, changing
its name to La Florida. Its reputation for tropical
juice beverages must have continued when Don
Narciso Parera took ownership, in 1898, and
even when bartender Constante Ribalaigua Vert
succeeded him. Because the blend of rum and
pineapple appeared more than once on its menu:

FUEGO LIQUIDO

1 ounce pineapple juice
Juice of ½ lemon
1 ½ ounce Carta Oro Bacardi.

---

207   Canova, Enrique C. "Cuba—The Isle of Romance", *National Geographic*,
September 1933.

Shake with cracked ice fill glass with Hatuey beer
and garnish with pineapple and lemon ring.[208]

HAVANA BEACH (SPECIAL)

½ pineapple juice
½ Bacardi
1 teaspoonful sugar
Cracked ice.
Shake well and strain into cocktail glass. [209]

HAVANA SPECIAL

Another drink, the Havana Special, appeared on drinks menus that was of Cuban origins that replaced the grenadine found in Fred
Kaufman's Mary Pickford with maraschino—a
signature ingredient in Constante Ribalaigua
Vert's drinks repertoire.

HAVANA SPECIAL

1 ½ oz pineapple juice
1 ½ oz Havana Club Rum
1 tsp maraschino
cracked ice

---

208   *Bar La Florida* (Havana: La Florida, 1936)

209   *Bar La Florida* (Havana: La Florida, 1936)

Shake well and strain into a cocktail glass. Garnish
with a slice of pineapple.[210]

It's difficult to say that one thing has anything to do with the other, but it is interesting to note that when this drink appeared in bars, hordes of tourists arrived from New York to take the boats in Key West, Florida aboard the *Havana Special.*

Operated by the Florida East Coast Railway, this train service offered travellers first-class accommodations and radically reduced travel time to cover the 1,596-mile journey from New York's Pennsylvania Station to Key West, Florida. From there, the rail service's steamships transported passengers in six or seven hours to Havana. Opened in 1912, the 42-hour, all-Pullman-car service included fine dining and a lounge car. Air service provided by Pan-American Airways, beginning in 1929, shaved the total trip to 36 hours.[211]

Even though a Labour Day hurricane decimated the Miami to Key West segment of the line, in 1935, the *Havana Special* was in operation until 1960. [212]

---

210 Zumbado, Hector. *The Barman's Sixth Sense* (Havana: Cubaexport, 1981)

211 The Lawrence Scripps Wilkinson Foundation Collection of Famous Trains. "Havana Special, 10701C" (Harper Woods, MI: The Lawrence Scripps Wilkinson Foundation Collection of Famous Trains, 2012).

212 The Lawrence Scripps Wilkinson Foundation Collection of Famous Trains. "Havana Special, 10701C" (Harper Woods, MI: The Lawrence Scripps Wilkinson Foundation Collection of Famous Trains, 2012).

PINEAPPLE MILK

Journalist Charles H Baker Jr discovered an interesting twist in the Piña Colada family whilst travelling to San Salvador, in 1934, where he was introduced to Leche Preparada Piña ["Pineapple Milk"].

PINEAPPLE MILK

Pineapple, sun-ripened until good and soft, juice and pulp
1 Vanilla bean, 2 inch long piece; or 1 tsp extract
Good sound liqueur brandy, 1/2 cup or so; or white Bacardi
Milk, 3 cups
Sugar, brown, to taste; white will do
Pineapple is topped, pared and sliced off core. Then either chopped into small piece or crushed in a mortar until almost pulp—saving all the rich juices. Blend everything together, let be for two hours, and serve well chilled and garnished, if in the mood, with incidental slices of orange, pineapple, sprigs of mint, or maraschino cherries. It is a grand how weather potation, and has been known to cause chronic invalids to take up their—and other—beds and walk.
213

213   Baker, Charles H, Jr, *The Gentleman's Companion: Volume II, Being an Exotic Drinking Book or, Around the Word with Jigger, Beaker and Flask* (New York: Derrydale Press, 1939).

Obviously the palate for pineapple and rum with a creamy balance had certainly taken hold in Central America.

PIÑA CON RON MEETS COCONUT

Another new twist on the ubiquitous rum and pineapple beverage was reported, in 1950, to have its provenance in Cuba—the Piña Colada:

> Drinks in the West Indies range from Martinique's famous rum punch to Cuba's piña colada (rum, pineapple and coconut milk).[214]

Where did this correspondent find this drink? The official 1948 cantineros' manual contained only a non-alcoholic recipe for chilled and sweetened pineapple juice under the title "Piña Colada".

THE CARIBE HILTON PIÑA COLADA

Far more important than the first collision amongst rum, pineapple, and coconut in a blender is the drink's transition from ignominy

---

214   "At the Bar" *The New York Times*, 16 April 1950.

to ubiquitous cabaña libation. Who standardised the Piña Colada into the drink we all know today?

The Piña Colada has been described as sickly sweet, a dessert in a glass, a beginner's drink. But like many other classics, it has stood the test of time because in the right time and place, prepared properly, it can be the perfect drink for that moment. The time and place might be mid-afternoon in a South Beach hotel swimming pool, or on the in the shade of an ocean-side cabana flanked appropriately by coconut palms.

It is generally accepted that this creamy version of the Piña Colada was introduced in San Juan PR, on 15 August 1954, at the Caribe Hilton's Beachcomber Bar.[215] The resort was still relatively new. Opened on 9 December 1949, with its prime beachfront location and modern amenities, the hotel drew an affluent, international clientele: John Wayne, Elizabeth Taylor, José Ferrar, Gloria Swanson and a host of others stayed there. Joan Crawford even declared the Caribe Hilton's Piña Colada was "better than slapping Bette Davis in the face." [216]

---

215   "Caribe Hilton, Birthplace of the Piña Colada, Celebrates the Cocktail's 50th Anniversary" press release issued by the Caribe Hilton. Year confirmed through interviews with former Caribe Hilton staff. This date has been variously reported as 1957 in previous press materials.

216   "Birth of the Piña Colada" www.frommers.com/destinations/ sanjuan0323027721.html

According to the Caribe Hilton press materials, Ramón "Monchito"[217] Marrero Pérez invented the drink, saying that he spent three months developing a cocktail that captured "the sunny, tropical flavour of Puerto Rico in a glass."[218]

Ricardo Gracia, another Caribe Hilton barman who originally emigrated from Barcelona, was quoted in numerous articles as the drink's creator. A member of the hotel's bar staff between 1952 and 1970, Gracia explained that he was making one of his creations as a welcome cocktail for hotel guests.[219]

Gracia's Coco Loco was a rum, coconut cream, and crushed ice concoction that was served in a hulled-out coconut. One day, the pickers who gathered coconuts from the trees around the resort went on strike. The hotel had received a large shipment of pineapples so he hollowed out a few and served his Coco Locos in them. He loved the pineapple flavour and accentuated it by adding pineapple juice. Then he named the drink for the strained pineapple that he added.[220]

Hector Torres also joined the Caribe Hilton in 1952, working first as a bar back and

217   Monchito was also known as "Moncho" by his friends, according to Norman Parkhurst, former manufacturer of Coco López. Telephone interview with Norman Parkhurst, 16 March 2005.

218   "Caribe Hilton 50th Anniversary" promotional card from 2004.

219   Telephone interview with Ricardo Gracia, 21 March 2005.

220   Telephone interview with Ricardo Gracia, 21 March 2005.

then as a bartender. When asked who invented Caribe Hilton Piña Colada, there was no hesitation in his voice, "Monchito!" According to Torres, Gracia was his and Monchito's supervisor. As such, Gracia was undoubtedly present at the drink's birth.[221]

Miguel Marquez, who worked as a waiter, headwaiter and maitre'd at the hotel, also states that Monchito invented the Caribe Hilton Piña Colada. According to him, Torres had already taken Gracia's place as Monchito's supervisor. Marquez also agreed with Torres that most of these early Caribe Hilton Piña Coladas were served in tall glasses, garnished with a pineapple slice. However, he pointed out that some were served inside pineapples or coconuts.[222] Score one point for Gracia.

Torres also remembered the Coco Loco, though he recalled making it with rum, apricot brandy, coconut water and a little Coco López. According to him, the mixture was vigorously shaken and strained into a coconut.[223]

---

221   Telephone interview with Hector Ramón Torres, 16 March 2005.

222   Telephone interview with Miguel Marquez, 17 March 2005.

223   Telephone interview with Hector Ramón Torres, 16 March 2005.

THE BARRACHINA PIÑA COLADA

A plaque at the entry of the Barrachina Restaurant in Old San Juan proclaims that in 1963 Ramón Portas Mingot invented the Piña Colada. Legend has it that Mingot was too shy to approach a beautiful customer, so he created a special cocktail for her based on improving a pineapple, coconut, and rum that farmers and fishermen had enjoyed for some time. She became his wife, and true to all legends they lived happily ever after.

But eyewitness accounts from Torres and Marquez date the Piña Colada's birth and naming in 1954, nine years before Mingot mixed his love potion at Barrachina.

When asked during a phone interview who invented the Piña Colada, Gracia replied chivalrously, "We did. Monchito, me, Hector Torres, Carlos, Roger Lopéz, Enrique. We did. The Caribe Hilton crew was like a family. You want to know who invented the Piña Colada? Just remember one name: The XXXXX"[224]

As for the Barrachina's claim, Gracia said, "The bartender there worked for me at the Caribe Hilton before he worked at Barrachina."[225]

---

224   Telephone interview with Ricardo Gracia, 21 March 2005.
225   Telephone interview with Ricardo Gracia, 21 March 2005.

One claim frequently ignored by most cocktail authorities is that Coco López launched Caribe Hilton Piña Colada out of obscurity. This appears to be true. Certainly, the Puerto Rican Piña Colada would not exist, much less become widely adopted, if not for commercially prepared cream of coconut.

CREAM OF COCONUT IS INVENTED

A common cooking ingredient throughout the tropics, but very labour intensive to prepare, cream of coconut was automated and packaged as Coco López, in 1954, by Ramón López Irizarry, an agricultural professor from the University of Puerto Rico. Irizarry personally approached bartenders and chefs around San Juan, encouraging them to experiment with his new creation.

The Coco López company then continued to spotlight the Piña Colada in its promotional literature for over thirty years, spreading the drink around the world. It finally found its way into the *Mr. Boston Deluxe Official Bartenders' Guide* sometime between 1970 and 1972.

The Caribe Hilton Piña Coladas were not all made in an electric blender. During the mid-1950s, the Caribe Hilton employed 49 bar employees and three or four electric blenders, according to Hector Torres.[226]

He related the following as the original recipe and method of preparation if a blender was not available:

CARIBE HILTON PIÑA COLADA (TORRES VERSION)

A cup of shaved ice 4 ounces pineapple juice 1 ½ ounces white rum, 2 ounces coconut cream Combine all ingredients in a shaker. Shake well. Strain the mixture into a frozen 14-ounce Collins glass. Then add the shaved ice directly from the shaker. Garnish with a chunk of fresh pineapple. [227]

According to Gracia, here's the original recipe:

CARIBE HILTON PIÑA COLADA (GRACIA VERSION)

One fresh pineapple
One green coconut
White Rum One cup
Crushed ice
Pour the juice of the coconut into blender. Add a scoop of the coconut's jelly. Chop off the top of the pineapple and set aside. Hollow out the pineapple using a pineapple cutter and place contents in a

226   Telephone interview with Hector Ramón Torres, 16 March 2005.
227   Telephone interview with Hector Ramón Torres, 16 March 2005.

blender. Mix pineapple and coconut well. Add the rum. Add crushed ice and blend five minutes until creamy. Pour Piña Colada into the hollowed out pineapple. Make a hole in the top of the pineapple for a straw,close and serve.[228]

In Gracia's words: "It's very important that it's creamy. Some bartenders add too much ice and it becomes a sorbet. It's not a frozen drink. If it's frozen,it's nothing. Creamy, creamy!"[229]

The hotel did not immediately add more electric blenders when Caribe Hilton Piña Colada was invented. As Torres explained, "It wasn't a popular drink when it was first introduced. No one had heard of it. Monchito would make up batches and pour them into three-ounce glasses. Then he would give these away to customers. When they finished, they would usually order a Piña Colada. He worked hard to introduce people to Piña Coladas. We all did."[230]

Miguel Marquez said that Monchito and other staff members would encourage departing customers to remember to order Piña Coladas whenever they returned to Puerto Rico.[231]

228   Telephone interview with Ricardo Gracia, 21 March 2005.

229   Telephone interview with Ricardo Gracia, 21 March 2005.

230   Telephone interview with Hector Ramón Torres, 16 March 2005.

231   Telephone interview with Miguel Marquez, 17 March 2005.

Today, the Piña Colada is still the Caribe Hilton's most popular cocktail. And there are definitely enough blenders to handle the demand. The recipe has now been standardised as follows:

CARIBE HILTON PIÑA COLADA (2004 VERSION)

In a blender,combine: 2 ounces white rum 1 ounce coconut cream 1 ounce heavy cream 6 ounces fresh pineapple juice 1 half cup crushed ice Blend until smooth,about 15 seconds. Garnish with pineapple wedge and maraschino cherry.

Nearly all Caribe Hilton-style Piña Coladas are now made in electric blenders. Though the blender was invented before Caribe Hilton Piña Colada, its rise in popularity, like that of Coco López, runs roughly parallel to this particular version of the Piña Colada.

ESCAPE

The brightest musical spotlight that ever fell on a mixed drink was Rupert Holmes' infectious love song "Escape (The Piña Colada Song)" from his *Partners in Crime* album that hit number one on the US music charts in December, 1979, and January, 1980. This tune cemented the Piña Colada's position in the minds of a generation of young Americans as the ultimate casual, decadent, romantic indulgence. (As the lyrics say, "if you're not into health food.") Those twenty- to forty-somethings, interestingly, are now the forty- to sixty-somethings, who make up the bulk of the cruise ship business.

Holmes admitted that he had never tried a Piña Colada before he wrote and recorded the song. In fact, his original lyric had been "If you like Humphrey Bogart", not "If you like Piña Coladas". He felt that he'd used movie references in enough songs, so he considered using a drink instead. Holmes recalled his moment of inspiration, "When you go on vacation to the islands, when you sit on the beach and someone asks you if you'd like a drink, you never order a Budweiser, you don't have a beer. You're on vacation, you want a drink in a hollowed out pineapple with the flags of all nations and a long straw. I thought, 'Let's see, there's Daiquiri, Mai Tai, Piña Colada—I wonder what a Piña Colada tastes like…'"

This was the last song recorded for the album, and Holmes wrote the lyrics the night before the recording session. He sang the song beginning to end in the morning when he arrived at the recording studio. This recording was to be a "scratch track" for the lead guitarist to work from. In subsequent recordings Holmes could not match the spontaneity and energy of that recording, so the final vocals on the album were recorded the first time he ever sang the song.

The song started with the working title "People Need Other People" and was originally released on the Infinity/MCA record label as "Escape." The record company added the parenthetical subtitle later because people were calling radio stations requesting "the Piña Colada song". MCA was losing record sales because of the confusion.

If Holmes had never tried a Piña Colada, how did it come to mind? One possible source is Warren Zevon's May 1978 hit "Werewolves of London", which included the line:

I saw a werewolf drinking a Piña Colada at Trader Vic's / His hair was perfect.

The year 1978 was a landmark for the Piña Colada outside the music studios, too. On 17 July 1978, Governor Rafael Hernandez Colon of Puerto Rico issued a public proclamation, making the Piña Colada the national drink of Puerto Rico. Monchito attended the ceremony, as did representatives of Coco López, including Norman Parkhurst, who presented the bartender with a colour television set as a token of the company's gratitude.

There may never be a precise answer as to who invented the Caribe Hilton Piña Colada. Was it Monchito? Gracia? Monchito and Gracia?

CONCLUSIONS ABOUT THE PIÑA COLADA

From Pineapple Rum to the Caribe Hilton Piña Colada, it is obvious that the blend of pineapple, rum, and eventually coconut evolved many times over the centuries.

It is possible that Cuban version was created by a lesser-known, unpublished Cuban cantinero and became popular with American journalists who encountered it.

As with many other cocktails such as the "75", the Aviation, and the Blackthorn, the Piña Colada has a name that was applied to more than one drink by more than one bartender.

But its Cuban provenance as a cocktail is undisputed.

A CHRONOLOGICAL TABLE OF PIÑA COLADA RECIPES

YEAR	SOURCE	DRINK NAME	RECIPE
1783	Morning Herald and Daily Advertiser	Pineapple Rum	recipe not disclosed
1819	Modern Domestic Cookery, and Useful Receipt Book	Pineapple Rum	An excellent flavour may be given to it by putting into the cask some pineapple rinds. The longer rum is kept, the more valuable it becomes. If your rum wants a head, whisk some clarified honey with a little of the liquor, and pour the whole into the cask. Three pounds of honey is sufficient for sixty gallons.
1824	An Essay on the Inventions and Customs of both Ancients and Moderns in the Use of Inebriating Liquors	Rum & Pineapple juice	recipe not disclosed

YEAR	SOURCE	DRINK NAME	RECIPE
1922	Travel Magazine	Piña Colada	the juice of a perfectly ripe pineapple—a delicious drink in itself—rapidly shaken up with ice, sugar, lime and Bacardí rum in delicate proportions
UNK	Various	Piña con Ron	1 ½ oz pineapple juice 1 ½ oz rum Shake well and strain into a cocktail glass. Garnish with a slice of pineapple.
1920s	Various	Havana Special	1 ½ oz pineapple juice 1 ½ oz Havana Club Rum 1 tsp maraschino cracked ice Shake well and strain into a cocktail glass. Garnish with a slice of pineapple.
1936	Bar La Florida	Fuego Liquido	1 ounce pineapple juice juice of ½ lemon 1 ½ ounce Carta Oro Bacardi. Shake with cracked ice fill glass with Hatuey beer and garnish with pineapple and lemon ring.

YEAR	SOURCE	DRINK NAME	RECIPE
1936	Bar La Florida	Havana Beach (Special)	½ pineapple juice ½ Bacardi 1 teaspoonful sugar Cracked ice. Shake well and strain into cocktail glass.
1934	Gentleman's Companion	Pineapple Milk	Pineapple, sun-ripened until good and soft, juice and pulp 1 Vanilla bean, 2 inch long piece; or 1 tsp extract Good sound liqueur brandy, 1/2 cup or so; or white Bacardi Milk, 3 cups Sugar, brown, to taste; white will do Pineapple is topped, pared and sliced off core. Then either chopped into small piece or crushed in a mortar until almost pulp—saving all the rich juices. Blend everything together, let be for two hours, and serve well chilled and garnished, if in the mood, with incidental slices of orange, pineapple, sprigs of mint, or maraschino cherries.
1950	The New York Times	Piña Colada	rum, pineapple and coconut milk

YEAR	SOURCE	DRINK NAME	RECIPE
1954	Hector Torres	Caribe Hilton Piña Colada	A cup of shaved ice 4 ounces pineapple juice 1 ½ ounces white rum, 2 ounces coconut cream Combine all ingredients in a shaker. Shake well. Strain the mixture into a frozen 14-ounce Collins glass. Then add the shaved ice directly from the shaker. Garnish with a chunk of fresh pineapple.
1954	Ricardo Gracia	Caribe Hilton Piña Colada	One fresh pineapple One green coconut White Rum One cup Crushed ice Pour the juice of the coconut into blender. Add a scoop of the coconut's jelly. Chop off the top of the pineapple and set aside. Hollow out the pineapple using a pineapple cutter and place contents in a blender. Mix pineapple and coconut well. Add the rum. Add crushed ice and blend five minutes until creamy. Pour Piña Colada into the hollowed out pineapple. Make a hole in the top of the pineapple for a straw,close and serve.

YEAR	SOURCE	DRINK NAME	RECIPE
2005	Caribe Hilton	Caribe Hilton Piña Colada	In a blender, combine: 2 ounces white rum 1 ounce coconut cream 1 ounce heavy cream 6 ounces fresh pineapple juice 1 half cup crushed ice Blend until smooth, about 15 seconds. Garnish with pineapple wedge and maraschino cherry.

Chapter 16
★ ★ ★ ★

And All the Rest
The Legacy of Cuban Cocktails

Any and every culture is best defined by its living traditions, those beliefs and practices that are passed down from one generation to the next. And in Cuba, the art of the cantineros conveys the same passion and vibrancy as a living tradition as the island's music, art, film, and literature.

As mentioned at the opening of this book, Cuba has always welcomed the new and different found in each visitor. Cuban culture, at its heart, is founded on adopting, assimilating, and embracing each new influence and making it wholly Cuban. The passion and beauty that is expressed from weaving so many threads into this cultural fabric excites each and very visitor. In turn, no one walks away from Cuba without becoming an ambassador, spreading its living traditions around the globe.

The body of the cantineros' art is deeper than the sea. And although we only discussed at length the most famous drinks from this living tradition, we will finish with a litany of 83 Cuban originals—from the island's Golden Age of Cocktail—that the cantineros are still proud to call their own: more than two-thirds of what every journeyman cantinero had to know how to make by memory.

To better demonstrate the transition from drinks made during the years of multi-cultural influence and drinks created when the early generations of Cuban-born cantineros came into their own, recipes marked with a star (★) were found in pre-1930s Cuban cocktail book. Recipes marked with two asterisks (★★) were found in circa 1930s Cuban cocktail books. The remaining recipes come from the cantineros' 1948 bartending manual.

A PIE

1/8 Apricot brandy
3/8 vermouth Chambery
4/8 rum
Juice of half a lemon
Shake.

★ ALMENDARES

2/3 English gin
1/3 French vermouth
Dashes of Jerez Domecq La Ina
Dashes of curaçao
Shake well.

★ ★ APERITAL

2 ounces Aperital Delor
The peel on an unripe lemon
1 Teaspooful Grenadine
Cracked ice
Shake well and serve with-
out straining.

AUTO

1/3 French vermouth
1/3 Old tom gin
1/3 Scotch whisky
Shake.

BACARDÍ

(see Chapter 13)

BOWMAN

1/2 orange juice
1/2 Scotch whisky
A little sugar
Mint
Shake and serve.

CABALLITO

1 lemon wedge
1 teaspoon sugar
Sprigs of hierbabuena
1/2 wineglass rum
1/2 wineglass Italian vermouth
Shake, strain, and serve.

★ ★ CAFÉ

1 Black Coffee
1/2 Creme Cacao
1/2 Soberano Brandy
1 Teaspoonful Sugar
1 Lemon Peel
Cracked ice
Shake well and strain into
cocktail glass.

★ ★ CAFFERY SPECIAL

2 ounces Sloe Gin

1 Teaspoonful orange juice

1 Teaspoonful apricot brandy

1/2 Teaspoonful grendaine syrup

Plenty ice. Ice a 6-oz. cognac glass. Serve w ith slices
of pineapple and two cherries.

★ ★ CALEDONIA

1/3 Creme de Cacao

1/3 Sánchez Romate Brandy

1/3 Fresh sweet milk

The Yolk of 1 Egg

1 Dash Angostura bitters

1 Lemon Peel

Crushed ice.

Shake well and strain. Serve
in cocktail glass with cinnamon on top.

★ ★ CASIANO

2 ounces Martini Rossi Vermouth

1 Teaspoonful Creme Cassis

1 Lemon Peel

Cracked ice

Shake and strain then, serve.

CASINO

1/2 rum

1/2 lemon juice

Dashes of anisette

Shake.

CHAPARRA

1 lemon peel
1/2 Italian vermouth
1/2 rum
Stir and strain.

★ COLONIAL (O MILLER)

1/2 maraschino liqueur
Glass of Old Tom gin
Glass of grapefruit juice
Shake well and serve in a wine glass.

CHOCOLATE

Juice of a lemon
1/2 glass of Domecq Tres Cepas
1/2 glass of Port wine
1/3 glass of raspberry syrup
Glass with chipped ice and fruit.

CUBA LIBRE

(see Chapter 12)

DAIQUIRÍ

(see Chapter 13)

★ ★ DELIO NÚÑEZ

1/3 Grapefruit Juice
1/2 Gordon's Gin
1/2 Teaspoonful sugar

1 Teaspoonful maraschino
Half of the white of an egg
Cracked ice.
Shake well ands train into a cocktail glass.

DOROTHY GISH

(see Chapter 5)

EL MUNDO #1

1 teaspoon grenadine
Juice of a lemon
1 wineglass Bourbon

★ EL PRESIDENTE

(see Chapter 4)

ELÍXIR

2 parts gin
1 part crème de menthe
1 part maraschino
1 1 part brandy
Stir, strain, and serve.

FLORIDA SPECIAL

I/4 orange juice
1/4 rum
splash red curaçao
dashes of maraschino
Shake, strain, and serve.

★ ★ FLORIDITA SPECIAL

1/3 White Label Whiskey

1/3 Martini Rossi Vermouth

1 Teaspoonful Amer Picon

1/2 Teaspoonful Curaçao

1/2 Teaspoonful Sugar

1 Dash Angostura bitters

1 Small Lemon Peel

Cracked ice.

Shaked well and strain into cocktail glass.

FORESTIER

1/3 dry gin

1/3 crème de cacao

1/3 cream

1 teaspoon Cointreau

Shake, strain, and serve.

★ HABANA BEACH

(see Chapter 15)

HABANA YACHT CLUB

1/3 Italian vermouth

1/3 French vermouth

1/3 dry gin

juice of 1/4 orange

1 teaspoon grenadine

Shake, strain, and serve.

★ HABANA SPECIAL

(see Chapter 15)

★ GUGGENHEIM

Glass of French vermouth
2 dashes Fernet-Branca
Dash of orange bitters
Shake, strain and serve.

★ IDEAL

1/3 Italian vermouth
1/3 French vermouth
1/3 Gordon's gin
3 dashes maraschino liqueur
6 dashes grapefruit juice
Shake, strain and add an almond.

ISLE OF PINES

2 oz grapefruit juice
1 1/2 oz rum
Cracked ice
Stir and strain into a cocktail glass.

★ JAI ALAI

1/3 Gordon's gin
2/3 Italian vermouth
1 lemon wedge
1 teaspoon sugar
Fill up with mineral water. Stir and serve.

JAIMANITAS

1 wineglass rum
1 egg white
Juice of 1/2 lemon
Dashes of Triple Sec
1 teaspoon grenadine
Shake well, strain, and serve.

LARGO

1/2 Italian vermouth
1/2 rye whisky
1/2 teaspoon sugar
Dashes of Amer Picón
Shake, strain, and serve.

LOBO DEL MAR

1/2 rum
1/2 dry Jerez brandy
Dashes of curaçao
Stir, strain, and serve.

★ MARAGATO SPECIAL

(see Chapter 3)

★ MARY PICKFORD

(see Chapter 5)

★ MAZAGRAN

Large glass filled with cracked ice.
Cup of brewed coffee
1 teaspoon sugar
1/2 wineglass rum
4 dashes lemon juice

MÉNDEZ VIGO

1 wineglass cognac
1 teaspoon sugar
Juice of 1/2 lemon
Stir, strain, and serve

MÉNENDEZ

Juice of 1/2 orange
1 teaspoon pineapple juice
1/2 wineglass rum
1/2 French vermouth
Shake, strain, and serve.

★ ★ MOFUCO

2 oz rum
1 lemon peel
1 teaspoonful sugar
1 Dash Angostura Bitters
1 Whole egg
Shake very well with plenty
ice and strain.

★ MOJITO

(see Chapter 14)

★ MOJO CRIOLLO

(see Chapter 14)

★ ★ MONJITA

Use a 6-ounce glass.
Cracked ice.
1/2 sparkling water Canada Dry
1/2 Anís del Mono (either dry or sweet)

★ NACIONAL

(see Chapter 4)

1930

1/2 teaspoon sugar
1/2 Italian vermouth
1/2 sloe gin
Lemon peel
Shake, strain, and serve.

★ OBISPO

A glass of Jamaican rum
A teaspoon of syrup
A teaspoon of red wine
Dashes of lemon
Shake well.

★ OJÉN

Glass of Ojen in a large glass with ice. Slowly add seltzer water and stir with a spoon until the glass freezes and the cocktail is made. Add a few dashes of Angostura Bitters and strain in a cocktail glass.

★ PERFECTO

Use a large glass
4 pieces of ice
Dash of lemon juice
Lump of sugar
2 slices of pineapple
Dash of Angostura Bitters
Fill glass with Champagne. Decorate with fruit.

PERIODISTA

1 wineglass rum
1/4 apricot brandy
1/4 curaçao
1/4 small lemon
1/4 teaspoon sugar
Shake, strain, and serve. Garnish with a lemon peel.

PLAYA MARIANAO

1/3 lemon juice
1/3 English gin
1/3 apricot brandy
5 dashes grenadine
Shake well.

PLAZA HOTEL

1/4 Italian vermouth
3/4 English gin
A slice of pineapple
Shake.

★ PRESIDENTE MENOCAL

(see Chapter 4)

REMERO SPECIAL

1/2 rum.
1/2 Italian vermouth
Dashes of curaçao
Stir, strain, and serve. Garnish with a lemon wedge.

RENE MORALES

1 teaspoon grenadine
1/3 dry gin
1/3 French vermouth
1/3 Italian vermouth
1 whole egg
Shake, strain, and serve.

ROBÍN

1 wineglass Scotch whisky
Dashes of Calisaya
Stir, strain, and serve.

RON PUNCH

Juice of 1/2 lemon

Teaspoon of sugar

Glass of Cuban rum

Dashes of Domecq cognac

Shake, strain into a glass adorned with fruit.

SANTA MARTA

Muddle a spoonful of sugar and half a lemon. Add 1
wineglass rum and dashes of kirsch.

Shake, strain, and serve.

★ ★ SEVILLANA

1 Dash Angostura

1/2 teaspoonful curaçao

1/2 teaspoonful sugar

1/2 Martini Rossi Vermouth

1/2 Bols Gin

Several sprigs of peppermint

1 lemon peel unsqueezed.

Stir and strain; then, serve with a couple of cherries.

★ ★ SLOPPY JOE'S

1 Part of Rum

1 Part of Noilly Prat Vermouth

The Juice of a lime

Drops of curaçao

Drops of grenadine

Shake with cracked ice, put In a cherry and serve in
Manhattan glass.

★ TANGO

1/3 Italian vermouth
2/3 English gin
1/2 teaspoon apricot brandy
Shake well, strain and serve.

★ ★ TEQUILA

2 ounces of pure tequila
Juice of a lemon
1 Teaspoonful sugar
1 dash Angostura bitters
Plenty of ice, shake well and strain.

URRUELA

1 wineglass dry gin
1/2 egg white
Dashes of maraschino
1 teaspoon grapefruit juice
1 teaspoon sugar
Shake well, strain, and serve.

VERMOUTH BATIDO

1 wineglass vermouth
Dashes of Angostura bitters
Dashes of curaçao
Dashes of Amer Picón
1 teaspoon sugar
Lemon peel
Shake, strain, and serve.

There are hundreds more Cuban-born drinks that were crafted by cantineros and their international array of mentors. And since it is a living tradition, there are bound to be hundreds more.

But that is the nature of a tradition that had a golden age like Cuba did.

INDEX OF RECIPES

F

G

H

I

J

K

L

M

N

O

INDEX OF NAMES & PLACES

X-Y-Z

ABOUT THE AUTHORS

Drink historians and recipients of the 2011 International Wine & Spirits Competition Communicator of the year Award, Jared Brown and Anistatia Miller have written more than 30 books during their 20-year collaboration, including *Shaken Not Stirred®: A Celebration of the Martini, Cuba: The Legend of Rum*, and *The Mixellany Guide to Vermouth & Other Apéritifs*. Their two-volume *Spirituous Journey: A History of Drink* charts the history of spirits and mixed drinks from 7000 BC to mid-20th century. (The first volume won a coveted Gourmand World Cookbook Award for Best Drink History in the UK in 2009 and the second received the same honour in 2010.) And in October 2010, the couple also received the Best Drinks Writing Award at the 2010 CLASS Magazine Awards.

Their company Mixellany Limited not only conducts masterclasses in drinks history and bespoke research for some of the world's top brands, their publishing division supports the work of authors such as Gaz Regan and Geraldine Coates. Mixellany is responsible for the Mixologist series of cocktail journals, republishing such classics as the *Café Royal Cocktail Book*, and translating others including the 1896 French tome *Bariana* and the 1927 Cuban classic *El Arte de Hacer un Cocktail y Algo Mas*.

Miller and Brown are contributing editors for World's Best Bars and are "cocktail gurus" on Drinkology. They are also regular contributors to Imbibe and CLASS magazines in the UK and Mixology magazine in Germany. They have written extensively for other publications including *Wine Spectator, Cigar Aficionado, Gotham* and *Hamptons* magazines, *Los Angeles Confidential, Boston Common, Capitol File*, and *Food Arts* in the United States as well as THEME in the UK.

Lightning Source UK Ltd.
Milton Keynes UK
UKOW030623180912

199177UK00001B/6/P